STO

The secret tax

The secret tax

What you need to know about inflation
(if we are ever going to beat it)

DOW JONES BOOKS
PRINCETON, N.J.

Lindley H. Clark, Jr.
Economic News Editor
The Wall Street Journal

First Printing, January 1976

Library of Congress Catalog Card No. 75–34853
Printed in the United States of America

1923464

Prologue and prejudices

L ate in 1961 I began writing editorials for *The Wall Street Journal.* I was fishing around for a topic, as editorial writers often are, when the *Journal's* editor suggested I write about inflation. That seemed a good idea. As a product of a conservative Midwestern home, I knew that inflation was a blight on the land, especially damaging for all of those widows and orphans and everyone else forced to live on a fixed income.

So I looked up the figures. Somewhat to my surprise, I found that the consumer price index, that figure so carefully calculated by the Bureau of Labor Statistics, had risen a little less than 2 percent in the previous year. A little dubious about the whole project, I told the editor what had been happening to prices lately.

"I know about that," he snapped. "Isn't it terrible?"

Well, I wrote the editorial and many more along the same line, inveighing against heavy government spending, large budget deficits and an allegedly free-handed Federal Reserve System that kept enlarging the nation's supply of money. Like most editorials, they seemed to have no special effect, aside from filling newspaper space. And as the 1960s slid into the 1970s we found that we had a lot more than 2 percent inflation to worry about.

For a newspaperman there are lessons in this, beyond the obvious one: never overestimate the power of an editorial writer. Back there in the early 1960s many people knew that fast-and-loose federal finance was sure to produce inflation. But it also built schools and roads, financed a war, increased welfare payments and stimulated the economy. It was easy to overlook the price effects.

Moreover, the government could do all of those things right now and the inflationary effects could be postponed until some time in the future. By that time the public might have trouble relating cause and effect, and even if it did finger the villains they might be already out of office. The public has never had a real opportunity to balance the costs and benefits of expansive federal financial policies.

Up to now, at any rate. The inflation by 1975 had grown so severe that nearly everyone at least wanted to slow it to more tolerable rates. There is no painless way to do so. The United States in 1974 and 1975 was in a prolonged and sharp recession that was sorely testing the public will to curb inflation.

Whether or not inflation is checked will depend very much upon what you and other members of the public say and do. Politicians will pursue an anti-inflation course only as long as they feel it politic to do so.

What you can do about inflation is, first, to support governmental efforts to end it. This book seeks to explain how we got into the current mess and how we may get out. Along the way it will offer some thoughts on living with the present inflation —and avoiding another one.

Before I plunge into this subject, I had better admit that I bring to it some prejudices. I studied economics at the University of Chicago some 25 years ago, and Prof. Lloyd Mints in his pleasant way persuaded me that fluctuations in the nation's money supply largely determine short-term price trends.

If that sounds a little like the gospel according to Milton Friedman, it is, but Prof. Friedman had only recently joined the Chicago faculty and had not yet begun to popularize his ideas. Incidentally, he has always stressed his debt to the Chicago tradition.

I have listened, I hope attentively, to most of the arguments against what now is called monetarism. Anyone who will accept the evidence of statistics can see that the correlation between money and prices is very close.

Some economists once were fatuous enough to argue that correlation could be coincidence. But Milton Friedman and Anna Schwartz, in their monumental *Monetary History of the United States,* showed that "coincidence"—if that's what it was—has been highly consistent over a century.

Some economists still argue that the causation runs the other way: growing economic activity, with resulting upward pressure on prices, causes the expansion in the money supply. Certainly it is true that growing business activity does press the Federal Reserve to expand money. But the Federal Reserve has the power to resist this pressure if it chooses to.

The Federal Reserve can control the money supply with some precision, averaged over a period of a few months, and thus check inflation and prevent its recurrence. The rest of the federal government can make this process much smoother if it keeps its own spending and borrowing within reasonable bounds.

Those are my prejudices.

Some of the material in this book appeared in different form in *The Wall Street Journal.* I want to thank the *Journal's* William E. Giles, director of management programs, for suggesting this project, and Frederick Taylor, managing editor, for encouraging it.

New Hope, Pa.　　　　　　　　LINDLEY H. CLARK JR.
December 1976

Contents

part three
How we may escape

part one
Where we are

How do you go about identifying hot grease?
You cannot arrest someone if you cannot prove
the stuff in his possession is stolen, unless you
catch him in the act of stealing it. And that's
almost impossible.

A Fort Worth, Texas, police official, quoted in the New
York Times, *August 17, 1974.*

chapter 1
What a mess we're in

Hot grease in Fort Worth appears to be one of the more homely symbols of U.S. inflation, mid-1970s style. Restaurants in the Texas city long have sold waste grease and oil to processors who use it in cattle feed; the stuff is stored in barrels outside their establishments.

Under the impact of inflation, the value of a barrel has soared from $12 to $48—and attracted thieves. Unless the police figure out a way to stop the thefts, inflation seems to be making crime pay.

The general public seems to regard inflation itself as some sort of crime. Public opinion polls indicate that many Americans think inflation brought us a depression, or at least pushed us to the brink of one.

For most Americans, though, such feelings reflect fears rather than reality. In early 1975 the country undoubtedly was in a severe recession, but talk of a "depression" showed that many of us have short memories. If we are going to return to the 1930s, we still have an awesome distance to go.

One man who is impressed with that distance is Geoffrey H.

Moore, research vice president of the National Bureau of Economic Research and a veteran student of business cycles. Comparing the 1973–75 inflation-recession with previous business recessions, going back to 1926–27, he finds the differences are considerable.

Those of us who lived through it tend to think of the 1930s as one long, continuous nightmare, but actually it had its ups as well as downs. The National Bureau, which carefully dates both ups and downs, says business reached a peak in August 1929 and then skidded to a trough or low point by March 1933.

From March 1933 to May 1937 things were getting better—not good, but better. Unemployment, which reached a staggering 25 percent of the labor force in 1933, had improved to "only" 14 percent by 1937. But then the bottom seemed to drop out again for a year or so. After the 1937–38 episode business resumed its slow gains until World War II brought a boom.

In the National Bureau's chronology, then, the depression of the 1930s encompassed two recessions—1929–33 and 1937–38, as well as two periods of recovery. Both of the recessions-within-a-depression were bad, but 1929–33 was really lousy.

Mr. Moore uses a table to measure the depth, duration, and diffusion of the several business contractions, and in every way 1929–33 was the worst. The contraction lasted more than three and a half years; the next longest went on for only a little over a year.

Depth? The gross national product fell by nearly 50 percent and industrial production dropped by more than 50 percent. Both figures are much higher than those for any of the other recessions in the past half century. The only figure that compares with 1933's jobless rate of 25 percent was the 20 percent reached in the sharp 1937–38 setback.

In almost every business downturn there are at least a few industries that continue doing fairly well. Not so in 1929–33: By mid-1933 every single nonfarm industry was reporting declines in employment. The next-worst figure was 97 percent in 1937–38.

Dreary as such figures are, they don't begin to tell the story in its full horror. Businesses and banks failed by the thousands; millions lost all the money they had and had no prospect of earning more.

No, we're not in a depression or even close to one. There are serious problems, all of them related in one way or another to inflation. The housing industry in 1974 was having something like a private depression of its own, as high prices and high interest rates discouraged potential customers. Meanwhile the savings and loan associations and savings banks, which provide most housing credit, found they could not offer interest rates high enough to attract new funds from savers.

High gasoline prices and high automobile prices combined to make Americans less eager to trade in their old cars for shiny new ones, so Detroit was having something a good deal less pleasant than a boom.

At the same time, however, other key industries—steel, machine tools, chemicals, paper—were hard pressed in 1974 to keep up with demand. It was a curiously mixed economy, one that deeply puzzled the economists—until the decline accelerated in late 1974, and began to look more like an old-fashioned recession.

Overlying everything was the inflation. The United States has had severe inflations before, but they've been associated with war. The removal of controls after World War II brought a burst of double-digit inflation, and there was a similar upswing at the time of Korea.

Always before, however, the upsurge of prices has soon subsided. But not this time. Many economists who consider themselves optimists think that the United States is sure to be living with at least 5 percent inflation through at least the next decade.

This outlook is based partly on the fact that the inflation has gone on for so long, and imbedded itself so thoroughly in the public's expectations, that it cannot be ended without pain—in higher unemployment, in lost output, and in other ways.

Even that problem might be surmounted if economists could measure the cost of the inflation—and knew just how much pain would be needed to slow it down. Then they could make up a neat little balance sheet and let the public and the policymakers take their choice.

Unfortunately, no such accounting exercise is possible. The public, in all of the opinion polls, labels inflation a clear and present danger. But that does not necessarily mean that the public is willing to accept one more percentage point of unemployment, even if that would bring prices under control. Or even half a point.

In present society there are many people who actually benefit from inflation and others who don't suffer much. A prime argument in the past has been that rising prices do deep damage to the fixed-income elderly, but Social Security payments now rise automatically with the Consumer Price Index. A growing minority of workers have contracts that raise their wages as the cost of living grows.

In a general way, moreover, all debtors benefit from inflation. This is true simply because they borrow dollars that are worth more than the dollars they pay back months or years later. Holders of real property may benefit, too, as the value of their assets may rise more than general prices.

Inflation in 1973 and 1974 was accompanied by a sharp decline in stock-market prices, deeply eroding the wealth of middle- and upper-income Americans, an erosion that has not been entirely overcome by the market recovery in the first half of 1975. The market's troubles have discouraged equity investment, making it more difficult for businesses to raise the funds they need.

If inflation proceeds very far, of course, it can cause severe disruptions in the national economy: It feeds uncertainty, stimulates hoarding, discourages expansion. The ultimate cost could be far worse than a presumably temporary one-point rise in unemployment. But that's the sort of cost that's not easily perceived by the public.

Public officials have tried hard to get the message across. In a college commencement address in May 1974, Chairman Arthur Burns of the Federal Reserve Board put it in forceful language:

> The gravity of our current inflationary problem can hardly be overestimated. Except for a brief period at the end of World War II, prices in the United States have of late been rising faster than in any other peacetime period of our history. If past experience is any guide, the future of our country is in jeopardy. No country that I know of has been able to maintain widespread economic prosperity once inflation got out of hand. And the unhappy consequences are by no means solely of an economic character. If long continued, inflation at anything like the present rate would threaten the very foundations of our society.

Strong words. Dr. Burns went on, later in his address:

> Concerned as we all are about the economic consequences of inflation, there is even greater reason for concern about the impact on our social and political institutions. We must not risk the social stresses that persistent inflation breeds. Because of its capricious effects on the

income and wealth of a nation's families and businesses, inflation inevitably causes disillusionment and discontent. It robs millions of citizens who in their desire to be self-reliant have set aside funds for the education of their children or their own retirement. . . .

In recent weeks, governments have fallen in several major countries, in part because the citizens of those countries had lost confidence in the ability of their leaders to cope with the problem of inflation. Among our own people, the distortions and injustices wrought by inflation have contributed materially to distrust of government officials and of government policies, and even to some loss of confidence in our free enterprise system. Discontent bred by inflation can provoke profoundly disturbing social and political change, as the history of other nations teaches. I do not believe I exaggerate in saying that the ultimate consequence of inflation could well be a significant decline of economic and political freedom for the American people.

While most of the public is deeply disturbed by inflation, few Americans think of it in Dr. Burns's terms. In a general way most people, quite correctly, put the blame on the government, but they have limited faith that the government will solve the problem soon.

So what do consumers do? First, they adjust as well as they can. Americans are a flexible people, and although they may prefer steak to hamburger they have shown that they can if necessary make the switch. The early 1970s have seen many such adjustments.

A rental agent on the New Jersey shore reported that nearly all of her regular clients again rented summer places in 1974, but many rented for one week instead of two or one month instead of the entire summer. Many people unable to buy new homes have remodeled the old one. A vacation in the Catskills replaces one in Canada.

Even consumers who can adjust to higher prices are by no

means happy with them. Jay Schmiedeskamp, who conducts the quarterly consumer surveys for the University of Michigan's Survey Research Center, commented on one survey's investigation of inflation: "I've never seen responses with so many swear words in them."

Angry consumers tend to lash out at symptoms of inflation. A particular target has been the electric utility industry, which was hit by the Arab oil price increases on top of general inflation. Utilities have never been widely beloved, and this episode has done nothing to enhance their popularity.

In late 1973, with the Arab oil embargo in effect against the United States, the utilities joined in a public relations campaign to persuade consumers to conserve energy. Consumers cooperated—almost too well. Electricity use lagged behind expectations—at the same time that the utilities were being hit with sharply higher fuel costs.

The upshot was that the utilities had to go to state regulatory agencies to seek higher rates. The public's reaction was predictable: They had gone along with the campaign to conserve energy only to be "rewarded" with higher rates.

The privately-owned utilities must continue to build new generating capacity if they are to keep pace with the public's demand for energy—conservation or no. Funds for expansion must come from one of two sources or from both: retained earnings or new financing.

If the utilities are to have earnings to retain, their rates obviously must be high enough to more than cover their inflated costs. Equally obviously, they can't sell new bonds or stock unless they are earning a respectable rate of return on existing capital.

The utilities, to be sure, have helped to worsen their own

problems. Historically, many of them have done a poor job of anticipating needs for expansion, and as a result rates have been artificially depressed for years. The low rates hid from the public the fact that energy was becoming a scarce commodity, and this increased the utilities' difficulties when they suddenly began to push for much higher rates.

State regulatory agencies generally have guidelines to tell them what is a "reasonable" rate of return. But the agencies are political bodies, subject to all of the usual political pressures. In New York State in late 1974 one man was nominated for attorney general partly on his claim that the state regulators had been far too lenient in granting rate increases. He indicated that he would do a better job of "representing the people" in rate hearings.

The Ford administration tried to persuade state agencies to speed rate-increase requests, but appears to have had little success. Treasury Secretary William Simon warned that the utilities' cash problems were forcing cutbacks in expansion and raising the prospect of "blackouts and brownouts and, worse, economic stagnation."

State regulators, quite correctly, say the real problem is the inflation, fueled by past government financial policies—not their inaction on rate increases. No matter how fast they raise rates they won't solve the problem until or unless the inflation is slowed.

Obviously, we're in a mess. Equally obviously, it's a mess that is less than fully understood by most Americans. Unless we begin to understand what is going on, we may face some of those dire consequences that Arthur Burns talks about.

Inflation is an insidious and destructive force
that is difficult to control, and our nation and the
world now face an inflationary spiral
unprecedented in any peacetime period.

*David Rockefeller, Chairman, Chase Manhattan
Corporation, in a speech in September 1974.*

chapter 2
Understanding inflation

One of the most common definitions of inflation is simply "too much money chasing too few goods." The definition is accurate and often useful, but it raises more questions than it answers. How much money is "too much"? How few goods are "too few"?

Common dictionaries aren't a great deal more helpful. The Random House American College Dictionary, for example, says inflation is an "undue expansion or increase in the currency of a country, especially by the issuing of paper money not redeemable in specie." Once again, how much can the currency increase before it produces an "undue" expansion?

The dictionary's second definition is more helpful: "A substantial rise in prices caused by an undue expansion in paper money or bank credit." But even that seems incomplete.

Back in the 14th century money consisted of specie—gold and silver. At the time of the Black Death, the bubonic plague that spread across Europe, the production of goods and services and the overall volume of trade naturally declined. With the supply of money little changed, the prices of the available goods obviously were bid up to higher levels.

Money at any given time consists of what people are willing to accept in exchange for their goods and services; it is a medium of exchange. It also serves as a measure of value and a means for storing wealth, but it could serve neither purpose if the public stopped accepting it as a medium of exchange.

During the U.S. Civil War, Confederate currency diminished in value as the South poured out more and more of it in a desperate effort to keep pace with the accelerating inflation that its own money-printing presses helped to bring on. Still, the currency was accepted, albeit with increasing reluctance, as a medium of exchange. With the end of the war the currency ceased to serve any purpose, except as a collectors' item and a curiosity.

Let's say, then, that inflation is a significant and general rise in prices produced by an imbalance between the supply of goods and services and the supply of money—the existing medium of exchange. Although detailed evidence is lacking, even for the Black Death era, there has never in recorded history been a serious inflation without a sharp increase in the supply of money in relation to the supply of goods and services.

America's first venture into inflation went right along with its first political venture: the Revolution. Congress had no power to levy taxes and the states were stingy with funds, and yet Congress somehow had to pay the army. Its solution was to turn to the printing press, grinding out growing amounts of paper money. By 1780 these "Continentals" were worth less than one cent per dollar, so Congress had effectively levied a tax on anyone unfortunate enough to get stuck with the near-worthless currency.

After the charter of the First Bank of the United States expired in 1811 and the bank went out of existence, the number of state-chartered banks mushroomed. The state banks had a high old time with their own printing presses, building up an inflation with their bank notes. The Second Bank of the United States then came along and pricked the inflationary bubble by insisting that state banks redeem their notes in specie.

After Andrew Jackson killed off the Second Bank of the United States, the state banks had the field to themselves. Some were well-regulated and well-run, but some existed primarily to issue bank notes. In certain cases the issuing banks were located so far from civilization—"out with the wildcats"—that anyone holding their notes had a hard time finding the issuer to demand payment in specie.

During the Civil War, both North and South relied heavily on printing-press money and holders of the Northern currency, understandably enough, fared better. But the Northern notes fluctuated widely in value, too.

A few years after the war, however, the Northern "greenbacks" were made redeemable in gold. The government in the latter decades of the 19th century was largely committed to financial restraint, perhaps overly so. There was a strong opposition, composed largely of Western and farm interests, that pressed hard but unsuccessfully for inflationary measures, such as free coinage of silver. The result was a long period of declining prices.

World War I and World War II both brought their periods of inflation. Until recently, in fact, the major inflations in the United States have been associated with wars. But now we're finding that war is not a necessary ingredient in an inflationary stew. All that's needed is an excessive rise in the money supply.

That, of course, is what we've had lately. The annual rate of increase in the money supply, defined as currency plus bank checking accounts, averaged well under 5 percent through the 1950s and early 1960s. From 1970 to 1973 it averaged about 7 percent. After continuing to rise in the first half of 1974, the monetary growth rate slowed sharply in the summer and early fall, as the economy sank deeper into recession.

Certainly the acceleration of inflation from 1972 through 1973 and 1974 was sharp enough to be called "significant."

To some extent, of course, significance is a matter for the individual. A 10 percent rise in bread prices obviously means a lot more to a poor family than it does to someone in middle- or upper-income brackets. In the past year or so, though, there has been little chance of finding anyone who would not consider the general price rise significant, to say the least.

Nearly all of the general public reaches this conclusion by looking at the Consumer Price Index. The CPI is computed by the Bureau of Labor Statistics of the Labor Department, and it tries to measure the prices paid by city-dwelling wage earners and clerical workers—not by consumers generally.

In part by excluding middle and upper income workers, the index assigns a higher importance to food than is true for the budget of the average consumer. That helps to explain why the CPI has risen faster than some other price indexes. Food prices also have risen more in cities than they have in some other areas closer to the farms.

The Bureau of Labor Statistics has been at work on an index that would more accurately reflect prices for consumers generally, but this project has stirred controversy. In a growing minority of labor contracts, wage increases are tied to the existing consumer price index, and some labor unions fear that a new CPI would mean smaller wage boosts.

The BLS also computes the Wholesale Price Index, which is

of immediate importance to businessmen and of ultimate importance to consumers. Rises in the WPI usually lead to rises in the CPI later on, although not necessarily of the same size.

There are major differences in the two indexes. The consumer index includes services which are not wholesaled, such as doctors' services. Imported consumer goods, such as Sony television sets, show up in the CPI but not the WPI. But imported copper, which may wind up in domestically produced TV sets, does get into the wholesale index. Retail price markups naturally figure in the CPI but not in the WPI.

The WPI has more downs than the CPI, since it includes the prices of raw materials, which can fluctuate sharply in either direction. Partly for that reason, the wholesale index tends to be much the more volatile of the two.

The third major price index is one the general public is unlikely to notice, except in highly inflationary times. It's called the Implicit Gross National Product Price Deflator, and its name probably helps to explain its lack of public notice.

Computed by the Commerce Department's Bureau of Economic Analysis, the deflator tries to set a price on all domestically produced goods and services. The price of that imported copper would not be considered, but the value added by the manufacture of the television set would be.

In general the deflator is computed by subtracting the value of all imports from the value of all goods and services consumed in the United States. A sharp rise in import prices, such as came with the devaluations of the U.S. dollar in 1971 and 1973, can appear to deflate the deflator. That's one reason why the rise of the deflator in recent years has appeared less sharp than the rise of the CPI and the WPI.

Assuming that you do want a precise measure of U.S. price

inflation, which index do you choose? If you're a consumer, the index that's most relevant to your personal pain is still the CPI, with all of its deficiencies.

If you're a businessman, the wholesale index is probably most relevant. But if you're buying at wholesale you will want to watch the indexes of the particular products you buy, which may be moving in ways very different from the general index.

If you're an economist you will probably prefer the deflator as the broadest index applying to everything produced in the United States.

Whoever you are, what you probably would most prefer is an index that comes down.

The response to disorder is unknown. We now have an Andromeda variable in our business cycle.

W. J. Fitzgerald, a Potomac, Maryland, economic consultant, May 1974.

chapter **3**

Inflation is everywhere

Some individuals, businesses, and institutions have such sizable financial cushions that even the recent inflation has caused no great problems. For most of us, though, inflation has been the straw that, if not back-breaking, at least has made the burdens seem much less bearable.

For a closer look at some of these burdens, let's visit Lambertville, New Jersey, an old town on the banks of the Delaware River. Down the center of the community runs a little street that seems to symbolize most of Lambertville's problems.

George Street, 8 blocks long and barely 20 feet wide, is too narrow to qualify for state highway aid. Lambertville, perennially strapped for funds, has patched the pavement again and again; the center of the street now is so high that rain sends torrents of water into the basements of neighboring homes.

"We've got to rebuild the street," says part-time Mayor Phil Pittore, a local shoe retailer. "But at current inflated prices it would cost us at least $130,000. Where are we going to get the money?"

Like most of the municipalities around the country, Lambertville leans heavily on local property taxes. Unlike income and sales levies, the chief support of federal and state governments, property taxes don't automatically generate a rising flow of revenue in periods of inflation.

As soaring prices push up local costs ("Blacktop costs more than $11 a ton, compared with $7.50 last year," says Anthony J. Nanni, the city streets commissioner), local officials have to push up tax rates. In Lambertville, a town of less than 5,000 population, that means socking it to your friends and neighbors.

"It's been damned tough," Mr. Pittore says. "What has hurt the most is that 18 percent to 20 percent of our residents are retired. These people are really hurt."

Many if not most of these retired Lambertville residents own their own homes free and clear. Social security payments keep pace with the rising costs of living, but many elderly citizens wonder whether they will be able to keep up with climbing real estate taxes. If they don't, they run the risk of losing their homes.

Inflation obviously pushes up property values, too, but that's not much help to older Americans. If they sell to buy another house, the gain on the first home is probably swallowed up by the price of the second. If they sell and then rent a house or apartment, they're hit with a capital gains tax on the profit.

The inflation of property values also is of limited help to communities such as Lambertville. Before local governments can capitalize on the higher values the property must be reassessed, and that costs money. "The last time," Mr. Pittore recalls, "it cost us $15,000." Even then, local residents can appeal new assessments to the courts.

The problem is intensified because tax delinquencies seem to rise with prices. In 1974 Lambertville set up a reserve of

$154,000 for uncollected taxes, $17,000 more than in 1973.

Some large cities, such as New York, benefit from sales or income taxes. Even so, as inflation heated up in 1973, local tax revenue rose only 7 percent across the country, compared with an 11 percent gain for the states and a 13 percent rise for the federal government.

The inelasticity of the property-tax take has caused municipalities to turn more to the states and the federal government for help. Recent court decisions also are compelling states to absorb larger portions of school costs; the theory is that pupils in poorer communities are treated unfairly because local governments with limited property values can't afford to raise as much for schools as more prosperous towns do.

Under court mandate, New Jersey moved early in 1974 toward taking over more local school costs, a plan that made some Lambertville officials ecstatic. "The state's proposal looks terrific," Mr. Nanni said at the time. Mr. Nanni and Mr. Pittore are two of Lambertville's three governing commissioners. In addition to streets, Mr. Nanni looks after recreation, while the mayor is also director of revenue and finance. The third commissioner, Elmer J. Sutterly, is also director of public safety. For wearing varied hats, the mayor is paid $1,500 a year; the other two commissioners get $1,000.

New Jersey's Governor Brendan Byrne proposed that the state pick up $550 million in annual school costs currently financed by the property tax. Lambertville was to get an additional $155,000, which was about 10 percent of its total budget. The state was to absorb 70 percent of Lambertville's school costs, up from 33 percent.

The trouble was that the funds had to come from somewhere. Governor Byrne proposed that the state raise the money by adopting its first income tax, and the measure made it through the lower house of the state legislature. However, defeat in the state senate seemed sure, and the bill was withdrawn.

That left everything up in the air, so Lambertville had to continue to struggle with its own financial problems. Federal revenue sharing has been a help, but it has come in amounts that are small in relation to a budget that, in 1974, totaled $1.5 million. In any case, Commissioner Nanni says, "Our needs seem to grow faster than new sources of revenue."

"We provide all the essential services that a big city provides," Mayor Pittore comments, "but we never have any money for capital improvements."

Even providing services in these inflated times produces problems. "Early in 1974 I was faced with a need to buy two new sanitation trucks," the mayor recalls. "But the trucks now would cost $30,000 each and repairs are more expensive too. We finally decided the cheapest thing to do was to hire an outside firm to collect the trash."

Salaries of city employees—there are 30, including both full- and part-time workers—have been moving up. "In 1973," Commissioner Nanni says, "the police came in with a lawyer for the first time" to negotiate wages. "The police," he adds, "were getting ridiculously low salaries."

Typical of the continuing squeeze is a park in the center of town, across the street from the city hall. The park has an impressive monument to the city's Civil War dead, as well as an old cannon complete with cannon balls.

There also is an old jail, which remained in use until a few years ago, when a prisoner hanged himself. Since then the police have been transporting any prisoners to the county jail in Flemington, a dozen miles away. There is also an old fire tower, no longer in use, that the city has been unable to find the money to tear down.

All of this is surrounded by a chain-link fence, topped by barbed wire, partly to keep local youngsters from climbing the old fire tower. The mayor wants to get the fence down and refurbish the park but the old problem remains: money. (He figures that once the fence is down he also will have to spot-weld the cannon balls "or some of them will come rolling down Main Street.")

Lambertville wasn't always in financial trouble. Founded in 1705, it prospered in the late 1800s as an industrial center. Among other activities it had a canning factory, an ironworks, a shoe factory, and a rubber-products plant which made "snag-proof" boots. Stimulants to growth were canals, on both sides of the Delaware, which provided cheap transportation; later, the Belvidere & Delaware Railroad came through town.

The canals still exist, but mainly as scenic curiosities; they haven't hauled freight in half a century. Trucks took over the job, and Lambertville lost one of its advantages. Rail service also declined under the competition of trucks.

Lambertville (despite its small size, it was incorporated as a city in 1872 and it remains the only official city in largely rural Hunterdon County) is crammed into 1.1 square miles by the river—which gives it a population density not much less than Chicago's Cook County. It has a lot of row houses, many of them a century and more old.

Some of the homes have been refurbished and are quite attractive, but some are badly run down. The city offices are on the first floor of a handsome Victorian stone mansion; the library is on the second floor, a location the librarian regrets, because of the community's large proportion of elderly residents.

In the lush Delaware Valley, Lambertville obviously has its scenic attractions, and some community leaders are convinced it can overcome its financial problems, even with the inflation complications. "We're going to pave George Street," insists Commissioner Nanni.

Americans do have a resiliency, an ability to absorb unexpected misfortunes and often overcome them. Although consumers tend to equate severe inflation with depression, they go on trying to cope. That makes it difficult for economists who try to assess what consumers are going to do.

In the final months of 1973 consumers already were well aware of inflation, but they apparently had more or less begun to adjust to it. The Survey Research Center of the University of Michigan's Institute for Social Research reported that "the steep slide in consumer confidence which took place during the first nine months of 1973 was arrested during the two-month period between early September and early October."

But in November came the Arab oil embargo, and it was a different ball game. Even before the energy crisis erupted, the Michigan economists saw no reason for great optimism. Attitudes toward business conditions, the economy, and government economic policies remained quite unfavorable, the analysts said, and they believed that their findings in conjunction with the fuel crisis suggested that "the onset of a general recession" was imminent.

The fuel crisis certainly did hit consumers hard. And anything that hits consumers hard is sure to hit the economy. After lining up for hours to buy gasoline, consumers were in no mood to rush out and buy new automobiles, especially not the conventional, high-gasoline-consumption U.S. automobiles. Moreover, that nice new house 30 miles out in the country began to look lots less appealing.

Michigan economists are aware of the mercurial nature of human beings, and they try to allow for it by basing their survey on hour-long in-depth interviews with a carefully selected sample of 1,440 persons. But they really weren't fully braced for the reactions they got in the first quarter of 1974, when the energy crunch still was on.

Consumer optimism all but disappeared. If the findings in the fourth quarter of 1973 suggested an imminent recession, the first-quarter results, if taken literally, suggested full-blown depression. The first quarter, of course, showed a sharp drop in the gross national product after adjustment for the accelerating inflation.

By the second quarter, though, the oil embargo had been lifted, and the lines had vanished from most of the nation's gasoline service stations. If consumers did not exactly see roses popping up from every gasoline pump, at least they were more cheerful.

The Survey Research Center found that sentiment had turned upward from the first quarter, although it hadn't recovered from the decline in 1973. Consumers were deeply troubled by inflation, but the worry was having diverse effects on their actions.

In the second quarter of 1974 rising prices had convinced many consumers that they should buy at once before prices went higher still. According to the Michigan analysts, twice as many survey respondents said it was a good time to buy as said it was a bad time to buy. Those opinions were only slightly less favorable than they had been in late 1972, when inflation was much less severe and consumers were generally much more optimistic.

Jay Schmiedeskamp, director of the Michigan survey, noted that the buy-now people were sometimes the same ones who were unhappy about their personal finances and were trying hard to build up their savings. Two-way consumers are an unusual complication for economic analysis.

Buying in advance can be a intelligent way to adjust to inflation if it's limited to items that are really needed—and if it's not overdone. In the Germany of the early 1920s consumers bought in advance, too; they rushed out to spend their marks before they lost more of their value. At one point employers were paying workers twice a day; the workers' wives would wait at the plant gates to take the money and hurry to spend it.

Workers' real incomes (after adjustment for inflation) were declining in 1974 in the United States, though not at anything like the German rate. The German inflation had destroyed the incentive to save; the U.S. inflation has made it very difficult for Americans to protect their savings against rising prices, but the incentive to save has persisted. And their real incomes began to rise in 1975, as inflation eased.

Increasing prices have boosted the cost of such absolute essentials as food and home upkeep, along with everything else. Before any consumer rushes out to buy large household goods or anything else he wants to be sure that he has set aside enough to provide for the essentials. Thus there is an urge to save.

The personal saving rate, the percentage of disposable income that remains after interest payments and consumption spending, is not an infallible measure of consumer savings. For one thing, it includes debt repayments, which don't provide extra cash for consumer emergencies. For another, it's a residual item, distorted to some extent by inevitable errors in national income accounting.

Still, it's the best overall figure we've got. Through the first three quarters of 1973 consumers to some extent financed beat-the-price-rise buying by limiting savings; the saving rate stayed relatively low. In the fourth quarter, however, the oil embargo hit and saving shot upward.

Mr. Schmiedeskamp thinks several factors will limit the rate of saving. One is that inflation is likely to continue to induce some advance buying. For another, inflation still pushes up prices of essentials.

The consumers' ability to save, in the sense of laying aside ready cash, also was being limited by their huge debt burden. Figures prepared by the Commerce Department showed that total debt service—interest and principal payments on consumer and mortgage debt—amounted to 23.1 percent of consumer disposable income in 1973. That's up from 22.4 percent in 1972 and it's more than double the figure for 1949. An indication of just how burdensome debts had become showed up in 1974 in rising delinquency rates.

Early in 1975 the public appeared to be doing a remarkable job of adjusting to disorder. Still unanswered, however, was just how much more of this disorder it could take.

Many of my clients ask me, "What recession?"

George Hitchings, chief economist of MacKay-Shields Financial Corporation, in August 1974.

chapter 4
Inflation and business

Inflation does peculiar things to businessmen. As prices rise, companies find they are making profits merely by continuing to add to their inventories; the feeling can become almost intoxicating. Everyone talks about the country being in a recession, and yet business profits go right on growing. In the general euphoria companies increase the dollars they spend on new plants and equipment, only to find that the dollars of course aren't buying what they once did.

It's confusing. Businessmen thought they were keeping their inventories under firm control through 1972 and 1973 and well into 1974. In fact, the inventory-to-sales ratio seemed to be unusually low.

Inventories have always been something of an economic puzzle, since they are subject to such varied influences. Stocks may soar because businessmen expect rising sales—or because sales are not measuring up to earlier expectations. Inventories may flatten out because companies can't get all the goods they want—or because they have turned bearish on the business future.

Business was certainly booming in 1972 and early 1973, yet Commerce Department figures indicated inventories rose by only $6 billion in 1972 and at an annual rate of less than $5 billion in 1973's first three quarters. In the previous decade, including the 1969–70 recession, stocks rose by an annual average of $7.6 billion.

Inflation was confusing both the Commerce Department and businessmen. Companies generally carried their inventories at cost, and that tended to understate that value of their stocks as prices continued to rise. Later revisions by the Commerce Department indicated that inventories actually were rising at an annual rate of almost $11 billion in the first three quarters of 1973, or more than twice as fast as the earlier figures had indicated.

There was no mistaking the inventory buildup in the final quarter of 1973. Inventories exploded upward, rising at an annual rate of $28.9 billion. The pace then slowed through the first three quarters of 1974, but it speeded up again in the final three months of that year as the recession deepened.

The economic impact of the inventory acceleration was considerable. In the final quarter of 1973 the gross national product, adjusted for inflation, rose by a slim 2.3 percent. This modest advance would have been a decline if inventory accumulation had not accelerated so sharply.

In 1974's first quarter "real" GNP fell by 7 percent, but this drop would have been even larger if it had not been for a sizable rise in inventories. In other words, the winter's economic downturn would have been much more severe if businessmen hadn't been adding to stocks.

What caused the speedup in inventory growth? Some of it was involuntary, related to the Arab embargo on oil shipments to the United States in October 1973, together with the sharp oil price increases imposed by the Organization of Petroleum Exporting Countries. Oil shortages and higher prices, with the attendant publicity, cut sharply into sales of larger cars, which backed up on dealers' lots. Production cuts by manufacturers, along with the end of the oil embargo, later helped to slow the buildup of auto stocks.

But autos weren't the only items that were accumulating faster. In fact, more than half of the buildup came from outside the auto sector. Some of the nonauto buying reflected the fact that businessmen, with prices rising, have to spend more to get the same quantity of goods. Some of it came from a simple desire to beat higher prices.

Still another factor apparently was that businessmen did not see a recession either in the present or in their own immediate future. In terms of current dollars, sales and profits of most businesses were high through most of 1974, and in the circumstances businessmen felt their inventories were tight.

The widespread feeling was that the slump of the winter of 1973–74 was all that was coming, and that business would begin moving up in the last half of 1974. But businessmen reckoned without inflation, and particularly without the Federal Reserve System's efforts to check the rising prices.

In the summer and early fall of 1974 the Fed allowed little or no growth in the supply of money. Business borrowing to pay for all of that inventory spending had already helped to push up interest rates and tight money kept the rates high. Scarce and expensive money began slowing the economy, as it always does. Businessmen began taking harder looks at their profits.

More of them began to wonder whether it was wise to speculate on inventories. Prices of some materials declined, showing businessmen that it was possible to have inventory losses too. If stocks were acquired only for use in a business, inventory profits were really illusory, since as inventory was used up it often had to be replaced at higher prices. Nevertheless inventory profits are taxed as ordinary income.

That's only part of the story. Businessmen each year write off part of the cost of their plants and equipment, on the reasonable assumption that the facilities will exhaust their usefulness and have to be replaced. But the write-off is based on original cost, not on the inflated price that businesses actually will have to spend on replacements.

According to George Terborgh, economist for the Machinery and Allied Products Institute, the result of inadequate depreciation is that nonfinancial corporations in the first half of 1974 overstated their profits by an annual rate of $10 billion to $11 billion. Since inventory profits in the first half ran at an annual rate of about $34 billion, inflation's impact on profits has been substantial.

Figuring inventory profits was a special problem for the Commerce Department in the inflation of 1974. The department uses a carefully constructed formula to separate inventory profits from operating profits. The formula was devised several years ago, though, when 3 percent or 4 percent inflation would have been considered excessive.

Both government and private economists think that the formula the department was using in 1974 was inadequate to cope with the year's huge inflation rate. The inadequacy became glaring in the third quarter, when the formula indicated that inventory profits had leaped more than 50 percent.

The finding was so astonishing that the Commerce Department refused to believe it and decided not to release the figure.

Department economists decided that a major part of the problem was that many major firms had switched from first-in-first-out accounting to last-in-first-out since the formula had last been revised. 1923464

Under first-in-first-out, or Fifo, a company figures that the inventory it first acquires is the inventory it uses first. In a period of rising prices, this tends to reduce costs and increase profits. Most companies still are on Fifo.

In the years immediately after World War II, amid the post-war inflation, the American Institute of Certified Public Accountants pointed out the virtues of Lifo. Since the inventory acquired last was considered to be used or sold first, Lifo held down current profits—and taxes.

Until recent years the argument never caught on; some firms switched to Lifo but later dropped it. Fifo profits looked good on earnings statements and, in any case, the general assumption was that relative price stability was the U.S. norm. Why change to an accounting practice that was designed only to cope with what was highly infrequent? Well, 1973 and 1974 persuaded many businesses that high inflation might not be so transient.

Early in 1974 the Securities and Exchange Commission expressed concern about company profits statements. In a vague way it urged corporations to reveal in their reports the impact that inflation was having on their profits. In mid-1975 it was considering requiring major companies to do so. There was little indication, however, that companies up to then were doing much about it.

The exceptions were the companies that finally elected to take the step of switching to Lifo. Many companies probably would have taken this step earlier if it were not for the fact that electing Lifo for tax purposes means that you also must use it in your reports to stockholders. Switching to Lifo in a period of high inflation meant a huge impact on reported earnings. One large corporation, for example, reduced its reported earnings from over $4 million for one year to less than $700,000. Naturally, the annual report that announced the change spent an unusual amount of space in discussing elementary principles of accounting.

In mid-1975 some companies were just announcing the switch to Lifo accounting. No precise figures on the number of companies making the change will be available for some time, but there's no doubt the switch has been massive. It's estimated that the change to Lifo in 1974 reduced reported pretax profits by about $5 billion.

A few companies, however, are having second thoughts. The advantages of Lifo obviously are greatest when inflation is accelerating, so interest in the change diminished somewhat in 1975 as the rate of price increase slowed.

Companies adopting Lifo and thus cutting their tax burdens obviously have more funds available for capital spending. Inflation increases the need for capital outlays, since long-run control of prices depends heavily on the economy's ability to produce and deliver goods. Yet inflation also disrupts and distorts spending programs.

As the economy sagged in late 1973 and 1974, spending on new plant and equipment remained one of the stronger business elements. It bolstered demand in the steel, machinery and construction industries, among others.

In the first half of 1974, however, some companies apparently accelerated spending programs to avoid expected price increases; that helped to limit outlays in the second half. In addition, a number of utilities cut back or postponed expansion programs because of the cost or unavailability of financing —both directly stemming from the inflation or from efforts to cope with it.

At the same time, the inflation was setting up a sort of treadmill for business. Outlays for the full year of 1974 were estimated at a little more than 12 percent above 1973, barely keeping pace with the inflation rate. Since capital facilities continued to wear out or to become obsolete, this meant that business in the year actually did little better than stay in the same place.

What this means is that the backlog of capital needs continued to be large, both in the utilities industries and elsewhere. Even before the energy crisis erupted, the capital spending needs of the United States were growing fast. Obsolescence of facilities results not only from age and changing technology but from rising labor costs, market competition, and changing patterns of demand.

In recent years, moreover, companies have had to spend increasing amounts to meet new antipollution rules. Paul J. Markowski, an economist for Argus Research Corporation, estimates that for the seven years 1968 through 1974 about 45 percent of the annual increases in capital outlays have gone for meeting pollution standards; the remainder, in several years, has been more than eaten up by inflation.

"What this means," he says, "is that in some years we may have had net withdrawals of production capacity."

In the 1974 *Economic Report*, the Council of Economic Advisers pointed up the impact of inflation. From 1948 to 1968, materials-producing industries increased outlays on plant and equipment at an annual rate of 2.8 percent, when the statistics are adjusted for inflation. From 1968 to 1973, as inflation accelerated, the capital spending of these industries rose at an annual rate of only 1.9 percent. All along, the United States has been spending less of its gross national product on plant and equipment than other major industrial countries.

For years to come, businessmen will continue to face the problems of inflation. Business will have to spend heavily to find new sources of energy—and to gear plants to use higher-priced fuel more efficiently. A General Electric Company study in 1974 indicated that the United States must spend $3.2 trillion, in terms of current dollars, on business fixed investment in the 12 years 1974–1985. That's triple the comparable figure for the 12-year period ended in 1973.

The 1985 that GE projects is not an ideal. It would be a year that would still have 5 percent inflation. The average annual rise in the gross national product, with inflation extracted, would be 4 percent between 1974 and 1985. And capital investment in 1974–1985 would be about the same proportion of the gross national product that it was in 1962–1973.

Reginald H. Jones, GE chairman, told a congressional committee that business would have to raise most of the investment funds, but "given present national policies and tax structure, industry will be very hard put to raise its share."

That will be true, even if inflation is brought down to 5 percent. The task will be infinitely more difficult if inflation is more severe. Henry Kaufman, partner of the brokerage firm of Salomon Brothers, stresses that the success of our financial system "has hinged largely on the willingness of individuals and others to save in traditional ways. . . . Inflation, however, will reduce this process as savers lose confidence in currency and become preoccupied in seeking inflationary hedges of their own."

Businessmen not only borrow from individual savers but draw on company "savings"—retained earnings. However, earnings have been shrinking as a share of GNP, even as inflation has been making them look better than they really are.

Inventory profits will disappear as inflation slows down. Until businessmen can see their earnings more clearly they will be cautious about stockholder dividends. Low dividend yields in 1974 were partly responsible for the depressed condition of the stock market. Low stock prices, in turn, made it difficult for companies to sell new securities to raise funds for capital expansion. Inflation-boosted interest rates also made it difficult and expensive for companies to borrow capital funds.

So the first and most important step toward assuring adequate capital formation between now and 1985 is to bring the inflation under control.

The roots of the capital shortage of the mid-1970s go back at least to the boom of 1955–57, when many businesses overexpanded. The future at the time looked very bright. The economy was pulling out of the post-Korea recession, and President Eisenhower and his businessmen's administration were in Washington. It looked as though the years of post–World War II uncertainty were ending.

Otto Eckstein, Harvard economist and president of Data Resources Inc., has noted in an analysis that the capital spending boom was a little slow in getting under way. But in 1956 outlays on new plants and equipment jumped 21 percent above the year before. Nearly all of that represented new production capacity, since in those days little was spent on such things as pollution control. Inflation wasn't much of a problem, either, at least by later standards. Prices, as measured by the broad index that is used to convert the gross national product into constant dollars, moved up by only a little more than 3 percent in 1956.

The boom didn't last; it ran into the sharp recessions of 1957–58 and 1960–61. Back-to-back slumps presumably increased businessmen's determination not to repeat the overspending of 1955–57.

Meantime, Europe and Japan had replaced their war-shattered plants with brand new ones, with a lot of help from the United States. Foreign producers not only took over their home markets but, with the aid of an overvalued dollar, moved aggressively into the U.S. market.

The import competition was broad, but was especially severe for processors of basic materials, such as metals and chemicals. Prices were held down, and thus the rate of return on capital. That made it tough to raise funds to modernize or expand capacity, and late in the 1960s the need to install anti-pollution gear added to the problems.

In 1971 price controls came in and threatened to freeze rates of return at the low levels of the 1960s. So when the economy raced into the boom of 1972–73, relatively little had been done for a decade to expand the output capacity of the nation's basic industries.

As Professor Eckstein says, the nation began running out of primary processing capacity long before resources as a whole were fully utilized: "This bottleneck in turn creates shortages in the succeeding stages of production: While the machinery, computer and other industries have the ability to produce increasing output in their own factories, they are unable to purchase critical inputs. The shortage of finished products, felt all the way to the retail stage, produces inflationary pressures."

What is astonishing, in retrospect, is that no one saw all of this developing in the 1960s. As Professor Eckstein says, "Neither business nor government was alert to these problems. Nor did the economists show more foresight. We are all accustomed to an economy dominated by demand forces and take the solution of production problems for granted."

Anyone who paid attention to the utilization of output capacity during the 1960s was likely to watch the broad index published regularly by the Federal Reserve Board. At the start of the decade this index showed that manufacturers were producing at about 75 percent of capacity. The ratio rose to over 90 percent for a time in 1966 but fell back into the 80s and, in the 1969–70 recession, into the 70s. In 1973 it hovered in the low 80s, a situation that led some economists to discount inflation prospects, since they felt that the economy had ample room to expand.

The *Federal Reserve Bulletin* of August 1973, however, introduced a different index. The Fed actually had been measuring capacity utilization in major materials industries since the mid-1950s, but the figures were largely for internal use. The figures covered basic steel, primary aluminum, primary copper, synthetic fibers, paper, paperboard, wood pulp, softwood plywood, cement, petroleum refining, and broadwoven fabrics.

The story the figures told was far different from the one presented by the broader index. By mid-1973 the major materials industries were producing at more than 94 percent of capacity, compared with about 83 percent for all manufacturing.

Professor Eckstein is clearly right when he says that "economic analysts and economic policy will have to give weight to these problems" in the future. What's needed is in part better planning by business to keep technology flowing and productivity growing. The troubles of the past years, however, are traceable largely to governments.

Our government and others, for one thing, showed too little concern for the worth of their currencies. Yet they clung to the fixed-exchange rate system, only occasionally devaluing or revaluing their currencies.

Fixed rates finally collapsed in 1971, and to the surprise and even horror of some bankers and economists, floating rates appeared to work tolerably well. They have eased the strains from soaring oil prices.

No one wants to reverse the anti-pollution gains of recent years, but perhaps in the future there will have to be more careful consideration of the broad impact of such programs. The nation needs clean air and water, but it needs a functioning economy too.

Most important, the nation must provide a stable monetary and fiscal framework for the economy if it is to minimize the inflationary pressures that we have experienced.

During the recent boom, some carelessness
crept into our financial system, as usually
happens in a time of inflation.

*Arthur F. Burns, Chairman of the Federal Reserve
Board, in testimony before the Joint Congressional
Economic Committee, August 1974.*

chapter 5
Inflation and institutions

Walking down Wall Street one day in mid-1974, a young woman was heard to reassure her companion that the troubles of Franklin National Bank, which had just reported huge losses on foreign-exchange transactions, were not going to wreck the economy.

"Yes," replied the companion. "But what if all the banks fail?"

Six decades ago the Federal Reserve System was established to prevent massive banking collapse. Before that time banks in some areas might be temporarily strapped for funds while banks elsewhere had more than they needed. Banks, moreover, kept their reserves in the form of deposits in other banks; if a reserve-holding bank failed, there could be a domino-like fall of other institutions.

The Fed was supposed to change all that. When banks need cash for seasonal purposes the system sees that they get it. And banks now keep their reserves on deposit at their friendly regional Reserve Bank. Unfortunately, it has taken the Federal Reserve a long, long time to learn its role.

In the early 1930s the Fed permitted a sharp decline in the money supply, helping to deepen the economic decline. Troubles of a few banks quickly spread to others as a worried public rushed to withdraw its funds.

The government's response was to create the Federal Deposit Insurance Corporation, which guaranteed the safety of smaller depositors' funds. Since then there has been no repetition of the panics of 1907 and the early 1930s.

However, there have been so-called liquidity crises, when banks or business or both have been strapped for funds. And over the years many people have come to regard it as the Fed's responsibility to pour out enough money to float banks and businesses through such troubles.

The Federal Reserve was supposed to correct the malfunctions of the old financial system. Now, it seems, the Fed is being asked to correct the malfunctions of some of the persons within the system.

To some extent the Federal Reserve's rescue missions are unavoidable. In 1970 the system couldn't have stood idly by, watching the collapse of the Penn Central trigger broader trouble. When New York's Franklin National Bank ran into huge foreign-exchange losses in 1974 the Reserve System had to try to prevent reverberations throughout the banks.

As one of the three federal supervisory agencies, the Federal Reserve also has some responsibility for seeing that the banks take proper care of the people's money. But a supervisor's responsibility is, or at least ought to be, to prevent mistakes— not to cover them up in a flood of fresh money.

In the past few years the banks have become less and less liquid, at a time when the need for liquidity has been growing. Inflation seemed to encourage speculation on the part of the banks, as well as their customers. This doesn't mean that the banking system became unsound; it simply became a lot less shock-resistant than it had been.

Banks moved more aggressively into "term" loans—advances maturing in more than a year. Even if all such loans are entirely sound, they don't possess the liquidity of the banks' traditional short-term loans. At the same time banks have tried harder and harder to be fully "loaned up"; business loans may not be as liquid as, say, Treasury bills, but they are more profitable.

Inflation permeates this process. Rising costs spur the banks and other financial institutions to seek higher earnings. Inflation pushes up interest rates generally, especially on the types of loans that are a little less than fully solid. At the end of 1971 the commercial banks' loan-to-deposit ratio was 64 percent. In the booming business of 1972 and 1973 the ratio shot up to 75 percent and in 1974 it moved higher still.

At the same time, the banks have come to rely increasingly on short-term certificates of deposit issued in amounts of $100,-000 or more and sold to large investors. These certificates are continually coming due, a fact that has substantially increased the banks' liquidity worries.

When Franklin National's troubles were revealed, the Federal Reserve for months seemed determined to keep the bank going. It appeared to believe that its responsibility went well beyond merely preventing the difficulties from spreading to other institutions. The Fed extended hundreds of millions of dollars in loans to the Franklin at its regular discount rate—an artificially low rate that was more than three percentage points below the rate the commercial banks were charging their biggest and best business customers.

The rescue effort failed; what was left of Franklin eventually was taken over by a group of European banks. The Fed, however, seems to have learned something from the experience. For instance, it now will engage in such emergency lending only at penalty interest rates, not subsidized rates. System officials also have tried to say that they do not think the Fed has a responsibility to bail out bad bank management.

The Federal Reserve's overriding responsibility, after all, is to try to combat inflation. That task is made more difficult every time the Reserve System has to rush to the aid of one institution or another by pouring out more money.

By standing out there as the "lender of last resort," as everyone's great hope in a liquidity crisis, the Federal Reserve may just possibly have encouraged some of the excesses that exist. Maybe the lifeguard will have to let someone sink to establish the fact that he also has other responsibilities.

Aside from the commercial banks, the institutions that most often concern the Federal Reserve System are the savings and loan associations. Like other American financial institutions, the savings and loans grew up in a climate of little inflation and generally low interest rates.

The associations originally were small community groups whose members pooled their funds so that some of the members could build houses. As the home builders repaid the money, with interest, other members could also put up houses. Since World War II, however, the savings and loans have become huge financial concerns, the major source of all home mortgage credit.

This institutional setup has always been highly vulnerable to inflation and the resulting ups and downs in the economy. As prices and interest rates climbed, individuals became less interested in putting funds into savings and loan associations and were likely to withdraw funds already on deposit; other investments were more attractive.

Savings and loans could not afford to raise their interest rates high enough to compete; they held large portfolios of old mortgages made at lower rates. In effect they borrow short-term funds and lend long-term money. So the savings and loan associations either lost deposits or gained them more slowly, and money for housing tended to dry up.

The Federal Reserve is quickly involved in any such situation. In an inflation, the Fed sooner or later moves to tighten money, thus tightening the squeeze on the savings and loan associations and the housing industry. One example of this double-whammy came in 1974.

The nation had just finished its three biggest home-building years ever. The total for 1973, even with a weak December, was 2,042,000 private housing starts, compared with 2,357,000 in 1972 and with 2,055,000 in 1971. No previous year had even approached such levels.

Even housing industry officials, after three such years, expected some slowdown. Overbuilding was evident in some areas of the country. The heating up of inflation and the rise of interest rates in 1973 made the slowdown certain.

By mid-1974 housing starts had declined to an annual rate of around 1.5 million, and many economists expected the year to wind up at about that level. But then the Federal Reserve really began to try to bring down inflation by severely tightening money. One result was to deepen the recession and increase housing's problems.

If the government tries to help housing by channeling more money into the market, as it usually does, it intensifies the inflationary bidding for resources and helps to push prices ever higher. This obliges the Federal Reserve System to squeeze even harder as it tries to eliminate inflation from the economy —and thus to intensify housing's financial troubles.

The Fed, of course, gets the blame—as well as pressure for solutions. Recognizing that merely pouring more money into the economy would cause more problems than it would solve, the Federal Reserve Board has sought better approaches.

In a report published a few years ago, the board made a number of suggestions. It proposed, for example, the elimination of legal interest-rate ceilings that sometimes make it impossible for would-be home buyers to get any mortgage at all.

The board also proposed various rules and procedural changes that would make it easier for financial institutions to invest in mortgages and that would facilitate the flow of mortgage credit from areas where it was relatively plentiful to areas where it was relatively scarce. It also suggested steps to shorten the average maturity of savings and loan assets (by permitting some consumer loans, for instance) and to lengthen the average maturity of S&L deposits.

But the board clearly sees the basic problem: "The most important single contribution that could be made to stability of housing production would be obtain better control over the forces of inflation."

Banks and savings and loan associations aren't the only financial institutions threatened by inflation, of course. The stock and bond markets can trace a lot of their problems to the same source.

Inflation heightens uncertainty, and uncertainty tends to discourage long-term investment. One of the uncertainties is the timing—and severity—of any government moves to counter the inflation.

Nor are financial concerns the only institutions imperiled by inflation. When Arthur Burns declared in May 1974 that "the future of our country is in jeopardy" because of rampant inflation, he said, "The responsible course is to fight inflation with all the energy we can muster and with all the weapons at our command. . . . One essential ingredient in this struggle is continued resistance to swift growth in money and credit. The Federal Reserve System, I assure you, is firmly committed to this task."

The Burns words shook up the bond and stock markets, but at the time the markets' alarm seemed a little unnecessary. After all, the chairman had only promised "continued" resistance to swift growth in money and credit, and thus at least by implication was saying that the Fed was going to go on doing about what it had been doing. And statistics at the time showed that the nation's money supply in the previous six months had been growing at an annual rate of about 8 percent—hardly "tight" money.

Moreover, Chairman Burns went out of his way to promise that the Fed would permit enough growth in the money supply to "finance orderly economic expansion." Surely the speech at the time should have provided little cause for concern.

A few months later, however, the address in retrospect began to look like a declaration of war. At almost the moment Mr. Burns was delivering it, the Fed was beginning to tighten up severely on the expansion of the money stock. The tightening was more severe than the Federal Reserve intended, but the result was that in the summer and early fall the money supply was rising at an annual rate of around 2 percent, compared with the 8 percent of the previous six months.

It requires no imagination to see the dangers that Mr. Burns feared. Inflation, for instance, is undercutting America's very system of government, forcing local and state governments to lean ever harder on the federal government. Inflation heightens the problems of all private institutions, compelling them to turn more and more to the public purse if they are to survive.

Mounting costs are tightening the squeeze on private colleges and universities, for example. Some schools have been forced to close and others have been taken over by state governments. This situation came as a sharp change from the 1950s and 1960s, when colleges couldn't grow fast enough to keep up with the influx of students.

"Many trustees and administrators seemed to think that they couldn't do anything wrong," says Charles Nelson of Peat Marwick Mitchell & Co., a large accounting firm that is a financial consultant to about 100 colleges and universities. "They thought they would always have more students than they could handle, so they should just go on expanding."

Colleges, however, have found that the pool of potential students is no longer growing so swiftly. The birth rate began leveling in the mid-1950s, and the trend since then has been downward. The number of children under age five actually declined during the 1960s, and this is the population pool that the colleges will be drawing on in the late 1970s and the 1980s.

What's more, the nation's 18-year-olds are no longer the sure source of students that they once were. The percentage of 18-year-olds going to college is declining, perhaps partly because of the end of the military draft, perhaps partly because young people no longer see college as necessary to the good life.

At the same time, the private colleges have faced increased competition from state-operated colleges and universities. The number and size of state schools has grown sharply and, as enrollment generally has leveled off, the state colleges have had more room and have recruited students more actively. And, of course, tuition at the state schools is lower—a special attraction to students and their parents in inflation-pinched times.

In the mid-1960s the private colleges saw none of this coming; they were still building classroom buildings, laboratories, dormitories, and dining halls to meet the expected continuing surge of enrollments. Then, toward the end of the decade, everything began to fall apart.

At the same time, inflation was heating up, pushing costs sharply higher. Student unrest over the Vietnam war and other issues discouraged alumni contributions. In 1969–70 the nation slipped into a credit crunch and a business recession. Many colleges had to borrow from banks to meet payments on those beautiful new—and often partly empty—dormitories, at a time when interest rates were hitting 9 percent and more.

In 1972 Father Paul Reinert, president of St. Louis University, estimated that one private college a week was either being closed or taken over by state governments. Later he and other authorities estimated that the attrition rate had slowed sharply, partly because most of the weaker institutions already had been squeezed out. But no one saw the long-run prospects as bright while inflation persisted.

"Many colleges still are looking to Washington for more help, but they aren't going to get it," said Alvin C. Eurich, president of the Academy for Educational Development, a nonprofit organization specializing in educational planning. "The period of the 1960s was one of great affluence for educational institutions. Federal and state governments were enormously increasing spending on education." Spending is still rising, but much more slowly—often not fast enough to keep pace with inflation.

For the foreseeable future, most education authorities agree, private colleges and universities will have to continue to hold down costs as much as possible. "Our theme has been, 'Don't build anything if you can avoid it,' " says Jane Lord of Educational Facilities Laboratories, a research organization set up by the Ford Foundation.

No matter how hard the schools try to curb expenses, though, inflation means there are some costs they can't control. The same applies to private hospitals, other charitable organizations —all of the private institutions that have been so much a part of American life.

Although governments have become increasingly important in the past half-century, Americans have clung to their private institutions. Now inflation may be loosening their grip.

The whole civilized world is now eager to know whether in the future the high cost of living is to advance further, recede or remain stationary. Opinions are plentiful but data supporting them are few.

Irving Fisher, in an article in the American Economic Review, *vol. 2, no. 3, September 1912.*

```
************************************************
*                                              *
*    YOUR NEW SPIRITUAL BIRTHDAY               *
*                                              *
************************************************
* Every human being has had a underline{physical} birth-
* day. But not every person has had a new God-
* given spiritual birthday. These two birthdays
* are not the same! If anyone has not had a
* born again spiritual regeneration, they will
* not go to heaven when they die.  Jesus Christ
* tells us: Except a man be born again, he can-
* not see the kingdom of God" (John 3:3).
*
* HOW TO HAVE A NEW SPIRITUAL BIRTHDAY:
*
* 1- confess that you are a sinner
* 2- be truly sorry for all of your sins
* 3- ask God to forgive your sins
* 4- ask Jesus Christ into your heart
* 5- have faith that you are saved
* 6- confess Jesus Christ before all men
*
* HOW TO ASK TO BE REBORN SPIRITUALLY:
*
* Dear God, I admit that I am a sinner and have
* sinned against your holy commandments.  I am
* sorry for my transgressions and I truly ask
* for your forgiveness.  I promise to live for
* you in the future with the help of your won-
* derful Holy Spirit. I now invite Jesus Christ
* into my heart as my only personal Savior.
*
* MY PHYSICAL BIRTHDAY IS:        _____
*
* MY NEW SPIRITUAL BIRTH-
* DAY (TODAY) IS:                 _____
*
* SIGNED:                         _____
*
* Put this new birth certificate into use NOW!
************************************************
```

chapter **6**

Inflation spreads abroad

In the years since Irving Fisher wrote the world has become vastly more interdependent, so that the inflationary policies of any major country have had effects reaching far beyond that nation itself. Until recent years the spread of the effects has been assured by a system of fixed exchange rates.

The idea of fixed rates is that the U.S. dollar is worth so many marks, so many francs and so many yen—so many and no more or less. The depression of the 1930s and World War II shook up the relationships among currencies. But in 1944, at a mountain resort in New Hampshire, world financial leaders tried to build a new and better world monetary system.

The so-called Bretton Woods agreement sought to stress flexibility: It included arrangements for regular review of the exchange rates of the various currencies. But in practice Bretton Woods became pretty much of a fixed-rate system.

No country was happy about devaluing its currency, no matter how badly its money was overvalued. To do so would be to admit the government had so mismanaged its finances as to impair the money's worth. Countries also were not happy about revaluing their currencies upward, since that meant that their exports became more expensive.

If a country has an overvalued currency it can solve its problem by deflating its domestic economy. Deflation will cheapen its exports and presumably help its balance of payments. If a country has an undervalued currency, it can inflate its economy, making its exports more expensive—and hurting its balance of payments.

Neither deflation nor inflation, though, is a popular course politically. The former is the least salable, since it can quickly push a country into a recession or depression. A country can more or less drift into more inflation without any announced program (in fact, with announcements that it intends quite the contrary).

During the Bretton Woods years, countries occasionally got together for crisis conferences that resulted in some realignments of exchange rates. Usually they tried to ward off such developments by supporting their currencies in the market or imposing controls on trade and investment.

The United States had a unique position in this situation. After World War II the dollar was much the strongest currency in the non-Communist world. The U.S. industrial plant was huge and thriving, while the industries of Europe and Japan were war-devastated. The dollar became in effect an international currency, and a key worry outside the United States was the severe dollar shortage.

Bretton Woods intentionally overvalued the U.S. dollar, in large part because it seemed necessary to encourage the exports of Europe once that area again became capable of exporting. With extensive and expensive U.S. help, of course, Europe and

Japan did indeed rebuild their industries and became highly competitive in international markets.

The fixed-rate system lacked the flexibility to adjust to the new order of things. As the keystone of the new system the United States felt that it could not on its own revalue the dollar in relation to other currencies, although it was becoming increasingly apparent that the dollar was overvalued. The non-Communist world was on what amounted to a dollar standard, since many other countries pegged their currencies to the dollar.

With some help from domestic inflationary policies, the United States began to run consistent deficits in its payments accounts with other countries. In theory the United States could have corrected this situation by embarking on a massive deflationary program at home, but such a program was never seriously considered.

Well into the decade of the 1960s, other nations were willing to give the United States plenty of room to maneuver. First, the U.S. holdings of gold, which had seemed oppressively large at the end of World War II, were nearly cut in half to help cover the continuing payments deficits. But gold wasn't always necessary: Other nations for years were willing to go on adding to their holdings of dollars.

For a long time, in international trade, the dollar was indeed as good as gold. It formed, and still forms, an important part of other countries' currency reserves. The outflow of dollars from the United States during the 1950s and 1960s, however, finally turned the dollar shortage of the early postwar years into a dollar surplus.

When the United States finally began to worry about its payments deficits in the late 1950s it began a long series of efforts to cope, largely through various forms of controls. The ties between the remaining U.S. gold and the U.S. monetary system were gradually cut, supposedly to reassure other countries that the gold would be available to back the dollar internationally.

In the 1960s, though, other countries were persuaded not to cash in on this reassurance by dipping deeper into U.S. gold. None of the maneuvers seemed to help the U.S. international accounts much, since they continued in the red.

There was one benefit for the United States in this process. As long as other countries were willing to go on adding to their own holdings of dollars, the United States could continue inflationary policies at home with less effect on the domestic price level than there otherwise would have been.

This inflationary safety valve became especially important in the late 1960s, after the Vietnam war buildup got under way. In a very real sense the United States did not have to suffer all of its own inflation; it was allowed to export some of it.

The rest of the world had a choice. As all of the dollars flowed abroad, the supply of dollars in world markets soon exceeded the demand. The natural result would have been for other countries to revalue their currencies upward in terms of the dollar to a point where some sort of market equilibrium would have been achieved.

Of course if the market had been free—if exchange rates had not been fixed—the dollar would simply have floated down to a new and lower level determined by supply and demand. But in the late 1960s the world was by no means ready to accept a floating rate system.

The world, in fact, was not ready to accept the sort of flexibility in fixed rates that could have made some sort of adjustment to the new situation, a situation in which the dollar was no longer scarce but was in effect becoming much too plentiful.

Other countries enjoyed their access to the huge American market. Rather than revalue the yen upward, and thus make Sony television sets and Japanese textiles more expensive in San Francisco and New York, Japan agreed to a series of "voluntary" pacts limiting its exports to the United States. Other nations not only accepted the inflation exported by the United States but in many cases added to it with inflationary domestic policies of their own. A notable exception was West Germany, which did revalue its currency upward and domestically did a highly effective job of keeping inflation under control. And it also proved that stable domestic policies were not at all incompatible with a strong and consistent performance in world export markets.

In August 1971 the United States finally lost patience with the world's refusal to readjust currencies to reflect the dollar's vastly changed status: The United States cut loose the dollar and allowed it to float in world markets.

Floating exchange rates, if and when the world finally becomes willing to live with them, would be an important step toward solving the problems of international inflation. Neither the United States nor any other nation would be able to export its inflation to others.

If the United States was offering more dollars on the international market than other countries wanted, the dollar would fall in international value, until the supply of dollars exactly equaled the demand. There would be no unwanted flow of dollars into a nation's currency reserve, inflating its domestic economy.

As the dollar fell in international value, moreover, U.S. exports would become relatively cheaper and thus would tend to

increase. U.S. imports would become relatively more expensive
and thus would tend to diminish. The process would not be
immediate and automatic, since price is not the only factor
influencing exports and imports; in international as in domestic
markets, people buy many products on the basis of quality,
appearance, delivery performance, salesmanship, and other factors—as well as availability and habit. But the readjustment of
exchange relationships would tend to work toward a new position of international trade equilibrium.

But the world obviously is not yet ready for fully floating
exchange rates. After the dollar had floated for four months in
late 1971 John Connally, then U.S. Secretary of the Treasury,
assembled an international gathering at Washington's Smith-
sonian Institution to reinstitute more or less fixed rates, devaluing the U.S. dollar.

It wasn't a good idea. Individual nations, especially the
United States, continued to pursue their individual inflationary
policies. By February 1973 the new rates were so unsatisfactory
that the United States decided that it had to devalue again.

Actually the float had been "dirty" from the beginning, with
various countries intervening in the market when their currencies moved in ways that displeased them. From the beginning,
too, there had been an unwillingness to let the market sink as
far as would have been necessary to soak up all the excess
dollars that were still held abroad. No one knew exactly how
large this dollar overhang was, but as long as it was there it
posed the risk of sharp market fluctuations.

It should be noted that some economists blame much of the
1972–1975 inflation on dollar devaluation. Devaluation, all
economists agree, has some inflationary effect. When the United
States reduces the value of the dollar in terms of West German
marks, one effect is to raise the price of imported Volkswagens.

But Arthur B. Laffer of the University of Chicago points out that this is only a nominal price change. As the prices of imports go up in the devaluing country, the prices of comparable domestically produced goods also tend to rise, until the "real" prices are the same in all countries. This effect, he argues, has become more important as trade barriers have been lowered among countries and the world economy has become more open.

There's no question that the devaluations had something to do with the extent of U.S. inflation. Most economists, however, believe that the devaluations reflected the depreciation of the dollar's value caused by inflationary monetary and fiscal policies in the United States—that the devaluations were more the result of inflation than the cause.

In any case, this was the uncertain situation that existed when the oil crisis erupted in late 1973. Nations were suddenly hit with unprecedented demands for foreign exchange to pay for the more expensive oil. Even many supporters of fixed exchange rates agree that it was fortunate that the world monetary setup had some flexibility when the crisis came.

Since the oil-producing nations tend to prefer payments in dollars, the world seems to have been shoved back on a dollar standard, the sort of thing the United States had sought to escape. After all, a country with a benchmark currency has a certain obligation to keep its financial house in order, something the United States has found difficult to achieve.

This new situation gave hope to some of the exponents of fixed exchange rates. "One may hope that this country has learned the lessons of its policy mistakes of the past many years, and that we will be determined to avoid those mistakes in the future," said Tilford Gaines, senior vice president and economist of New York's Manufacturers Hanover Trust Co.

"If U.S. behavior does warrant reinstallation of the dollar as the key reserve currency, most other countries that are now floating against the dollar will, either individually or as a bloc, establish fixed parity relations with the dollar. Maintenance of a fixed parity situation would prove to be relatively painless, even in the face of massive uncertainties in the years ahead, so long as the dollar remained solid."

It's certainly true that many of the troubles of the world currency system in the postwar years stemmed from the inflationary policies of the United States. And it would be wonderful if America henceforth would pursue a more responsible course.

Even if the United States does swear off financial excess, however, it's a little much to expect all other countries to do so. And the fixed rate supporters are a little optimistic if they believe that other countries would make the timely and small adjustments needed to make their rates conform with reality. History has shown that a fixed rate soon acquires a religious aspect and must be maintained no matter the cost of controls over trade and currency.

Experience indicates that nations can get along remarkably well with floating rates, even if they at times override the decisions of the market. If nations suddenly began to pursue wise monetary and fiscal policies, of course, it wouldn't matter much what monetary system we used: Anything would work.

In the meantime, nations eventually are going to have to agree to a few more rules than they have now. One area that may require more attention is the Eurodollar market. Eurodollars are dollar-denominated deposits in banks outside the United States. The Eurodollar banks then make dollar loans.

Jacques Rueff, the French economist who was an adviser to French President Charles de Gaulle, blames much of the world inflation on the creation of money through the Eurodollar market. (There are Eurocurrencies other than dollars, but dollars make up well over half of the total.)

At first glance the French economist's view appears to possess a certain logic. The Eurodollar market has grown enormously since it first got started in the late 1950s. An analysis by New York's First National City bank notes that the Eurodollar market, though smaller than the U.S. money market, dwarfs the money markets of nearly all other countries.

Moreover, the market is free of government regulation, except for whatever rules may govern movement of foreign exchange. In theory, since it has no reserve requirements, it could expand international credit infinitely. The very idea is a little scary.

Before assessing such fears, let's consider how and why the Eurodollar market got started. First, how did all those dollar deposits get into banks abroad?

A common explanation has been to cite the long U.S. record of international payments deficits. Unfortunately, notes National City, there is no stable and significant relationship between the Eurodollar market's growth and the cumulated payments deficit.

But the bank goes on to comment that "a fairly stable correlation does exist between the growth of the U.S. monetary base—the reserves of Federal Reserve System member banks and currency in circulation—and the growth of the Eurodollar market. And this suggests a different approach to the search for a Eurodollar base, one in which the Eurodollar is viewed as part of the U.S. money market." If this is the correct approach, and the correlation is very close, the United States has fueled the growth of the Eurodollar market with its own domestic monetary expansion.

Just because the United States creates a lot of inflationary dollars doesn't mean that the dollars have to show up as Eurodollar deposits. The fast growth of the Eurodollar market was a response to the money market controls imposed by national governments.

A country or a company often can invest dollars in the Eurodollar market and get higher rates of return than it could at home. Similarly, a country or a company often can borrow dollars in the Eurodollar market at lower rates than it would have to pay at home for credit in its own currency.

"Because they are free from the reserve requirements and other regulations imposed by the Federal Reserve or any other central bank," says National City, "Eurodollar banks can pay more on deposits, charge less for loans than their domestic counterparts and still enjoy a profitable spread."

But a nagging question remains: How about that potential for infinite credit expansion? So far, it hasn't happened. In fact, the Eurodollar banks as a group have been much less expansionary than the U.S. domestic banking system. But if the Eurodollar market continues to grow as rapidly as it has in the past, pressure surely will increase for control.

If the United States and other major countries kept their domestic monetary expansions under better control, the Eurodollar market would have far less potential for growth. And if traditional money markets were better developed and less hobbled by controls, there would be far less need for a Eurodollar market. A healthy step in this direction was Treasury Secretary George Shultz's decision in 1973 to ease curbs on U.S. foreign investment.

When the oil crisis came, of course, the Eurodollar market became an indispensable means for handling the dollars the oil producers were accumulating as a result of the sharply higher petroleum prices. The oil producers deposit dollars in the market, and the consumers borrow dollars to pay for the oil.

So far the market has seemed to work remarkably well. It is unlikely, however, that the world will indefinitely permit such a huge money market to function with no supervision whatsoever. Since the market is international, supervision will require international cooperation. How and even whether that can be achieved is, to say the least, uncertain.

If 1973 taught forecasters anything, it is that life
is full of surprises.

Argus Research Corporation, in a forecast for 1974.

chapter 7

Inflation blurs the picture

When 1973 began, all economists were looking for the economy to begin to move at a slower pace. The economy had been slow to come out of the 1969–70 recession, so the Nixon administration had imposed a wage-price freeze in August 1971, following that with a system of controls.

The theory apparently was that controls would make it safe to stimulate the economy by running larger federal budget deficits and by making credit both cheaper and more readily available. The recovery certainly picked up speed: For nearly two years the economy was in a roaring boom.

Prior to 1971, the nation had never built as many as 2 million housing units in any year; it built over 2 million in 1971, 1972, and 1973. The auto industry also had three super-years. Well before the end of 1972 it was evident that the economy was over-heating; although controls were still in place, the rate of inflation picked up significantly.

The stock market certainly got the message. Stock prices peaked in early 1973 and then headed down. Everyone knew that the boom could not be sustained indefinitely. The question was how far the economy would fall and how fast.

A gentle decline to economic stability, with levels of output and employment that still would be relatively high, would have been desirable. It also is the sort of soft landing that the U.S. economy has always found difficult to achieve.

The difficulty was compounded by inflation. Price increases continued to accelerate after the Nixon administration softened wage-price controls at the start of 1973. Some of the price increases were put through in the fear that there would be a new price freeze. The fear was well-founded; President Nixon froze prices again in mid-1973.

Crop failures at home and abroad put upward pressure on food prices. The pressure was intensified by the fact that most of the major nations of the world were in an economic boom. The phenomenon of simultaneous prosperity, a highly unusual occurrence, also pushed up demand for all other goods traded in world markets.

The world economic boom increased the inflationary effect of the U.S. devaluations. A number of U.S. industries, such as steel, were running flat-out and shortages were common. Capital spending plans were large and growing. In many areas the economy surely didn't seem to be on the road into recession.

Price changes varied widely among industries. For consumers, the chief worry was food until October 1973, when the Organization of Petroleum Exporting Countries reminded everyone, consumers and businessmen alike, of the importance of energy. Economists who were having trouble trying to figure out what the economy would do on its own now had to try to figure out what the Arabs would do. Would they lift their embargo on oil shipments to the United States? Would they agree to reduce the newly sky-high prices?

The winter of 1973–1974 was certainly a strange time. Much

against their will, automobile dealers piled up huge inventories of new cars—and in the process helped to keep the gross national product, in terms of 1958 dollars, from declining in 1973's fourth quarter. Inflation went right on heating up in spite of the new controls imposed by the Nixon administration in the wake of the new freeze in mid-1973.

But most economists thought this was a passing phenomenon. The general forecast was that once the higher oil prices were absorbed in the economy the rate of price increase would slow down. Interest rates reflected the optimistic inflation assumptions; short-term rates declined and long-term rates remained largely flat.

In the first quarter of 1974 auto makers sharply cut production to bring it into line with sales, and energy problems slowed output in other industries. With inflation roaring into double-digit territory, real GNP dropped at an annual rate of 7 percent.

But the general view was that this was just some sort of "energy spasm," which as it ran its course would take care of all that overheating back in 1972 and 1973. When the oil boycott was lifted, nearly everyone thought the economy would start heading upward once again.

Housing and autos were having their own depressions, but hardly any other industry even saw a recession. The talk was of shortages, growing order backlogs, and lengthening delivery times. Businessmen were frantically ordering materials that were scarce, or appeared to be so. After all, if they couldn't use the steel themselves they could always sell it to someone else. The way inflation was going, steel in the warehouse looked better than money in the bank. With frantic inventory borrowing from the banks, interest rates started escalating once again.

It's common to blame the Federal Reserve System for 1974's

sharp rise in interest rates. It should be noted, however, that the turnaround in short-term rates came in February. In February and March the Fed was expanding the money supply at an annual rate of around 9 percent, which hardly sounds like tight money.

The chief reason for the rate turnaround was that borrowers and lenders both began to realize that double-digit inflation was not going to go away overnight. Lenders insisted on higher rates to try to protect themselves against the declining value of their dollars, and borrowers were willing to pay the higher rates to get funds to build inventories that were rising even more rapidly in price.

Of course, a 9 percent expansion of the money supply when prices are going up by 12 percent still leaves us with a declining money supply, in real terms. About this time there were esoteric arguments among economists over "real balances." The arguments also were going on within the Federal Open Market Committee, the policymaking body of the Reserve System, so the inflationary confusion was pervasive.

What is the proper monetary policy when an economy is in a slump and inflation is persisting at high rates? The question brought a variety of answers.

Some economists thought that the Federal Reserve should expand the money supply at a rate almost as fast as the inflation rate, in order to make sure that the economy came out of the slump. Others argued that this policy would only guarantee continuation of the inflation and urged a much slower expansion of the money stock, even at the risk of deepening the slump.

One example cited by the second group was the German hyperinflation of the early 1920s. Through much of that period the German central bank explained its rapid acceleration of monetary growth by noting that real balances were continuing to fall. How could the central bank be promoting inflation if real balances were still declining?

German housewives would have had an answer for that when they pushed wheelbarrows loaded with currency to buy bread or met their husbands at plant gates to spend their pay before its value disappeared. Monetary authorities cannot afford to get in a race with inflation; that's the sort of race in which everyone will lose.

In mid-1974 the Federal Reserve apparently came down on the side of those who give limited weight to real balances arguments, since it slowed the money-supply growth very sharply. Even inside the Fed, however, the arguments continued.

Inflation also was blurring the picture by distorting official statistics. The National Bureau of Economic Research, a New York-based nonprofit organization, has spent more than a half-century analyzing economic indicators that tend to show where the economy has been, where it is, and where it is likely to go. In order, these are called lagging, coincident, and leading indicators.

By common consent among economists and government officials, the bureau has become the agency that decides officially whether the economy is in a recession, a decision guided largely by the performance of the indicators.

Until the economic decline accelerated in October 1974, the bureau did not see a recession. Geoffrey H. Moore, the research vice president who heads the committee making the recession decisions, said at the time that the "only aggregate that is performing as it has in past recessions is real GNP (gross national product with inflation extracted)."

Many analysts put primary stress on the real gross national

product. In every official recession since World War II, real GNP has declined for at least two consecutive quarters, and some economists now regard that as a definition of a recession.

But Mr. Moore and other bureau officials emphasize that they never have used such a simple definition. The bureau's analysts consider dozens of statistical indicators that they believe reflect the condition of the economy.

These yardsticks include such statistics as the average work-week of production workers (when it's growing, the suggestion is that companies are straining to meet orders and that business will continue to expand) and business expenditures on new plants and equipment (these outlays usually continue to rise for a time after the economy has turned downward because many projects take a long time to complete).

The recession decisions always are made with extreme care. The bureau, moreover, doesn't issue official progress reports on its thinking. In deciding whether a recession has occurred, the bureau considers the duration, depth, and diffusion of a business decline. In late 1974 real GNP was still the only indicator that was performing as it had in prior recessions.

Mr. Moore suggested that, in a period of high inflation, the adjustments used for eliminating price effects from the figures may be less than perfectly accurate. The inflation certainly does complicate matters for anyone trying to figure out where the economy is.

Although the bureau doesn't forecast, many economists use the bureau's leading indicators to make predictions. But several of these indicators, so reliable in the past, are badly distorted by inflation.

Take new orders for durable goods, for example. When new orders are rising it usually means that business is likely to get better, at least for a time. In a period of high inflation, however, the chief significance of rising new orders may merely be that everything is getting more expensive.

In an effort to overcome this problem, the Commerce Department has been publishing on an experimental basis an index of five leading indicators measured in nonmonetary units, such as the average workweek in manufacturing. In addition, Mr. Moore and other economists have experimented with indicators adjusted for inflation.

Finally, in May 1975, the Commerce Department and the National Bureau announced a greatly revised set of indicators. A primary purpose is to escape the distortions introduced by inflation, and the new indicators, if they had been available in the early 1970s, would have done a better job of forecasting.

The impact of inflation on statistics was vividly illustrated in late 1974 by the ratio of business inventories to sales. Throughout American business history inventories have played a major role in cycles. When inventories grow too large in relation to current sales, businessmen naturally cut back on their buying and start living off stocks. These cutbacks can help push the economy into a slump. On the other hand, when businessmen become optimistic about the future they start building inventories and their buying speeds recovery.

In the inventory-sales ratio, both stocks and sales are included in their actual dollar amounts. That seems a sensible enough procedure in normal times. In a period of rapid inflation, however, the ratio becomes distorted. The sales figure reflects the full effect of inflation, while inventories lag behind.

During the 1971–73 business boom, the inventory-sales ratio, not surprisingly, declined until inventories of businessmen on the average were equal to 1.4 months' sales. As the boom ended in 1973 and 1974, the ratio remained very sticky, moving up only slightly. The explanation was the high rate of inflation.

Through most of 1974 the inflated sales figures convinced many businessmen there was no recession; when they woke up to the facts, the cutback in their spending was sharper than would have been necessary if inflation had not so distorted the statistics. Inflation also made businessmen less cautious about borrowing, since they knew they could repay the loans in dollars that would be worth less.

Inflation also can encourage businessmen and consumers to speed up their spending before prices go any higher. Public opinion polls, however, have shown that the public tends to equate very high rates of inflation with depression and thus tries to curb its spending and save more.

All in all, inflation makes economic analysis a dangerous business for anyone.

part two
How we got here

There are few things more annoying to the macroeconomic theorist than to be told by laymen and newspaper editorialists, most of whom cannot solve two equations for their two unknowns, that the recent rise of the general price level is due to monopoly, or unions, or some other menacing economic power."

Edmund S. Phelps, Columbia University, at an American Enterprise Institute conference on inflation, May 1974.

chapter **8**

How we got into this mess

How did the United States get into its inflationary mess? The question is more than academic because, as Karl Brunner of the University of Rochester said in one study, "An irrelevant or poorly conceived explanation of inflation cannot yield useful suggestions for an effective and successful anti-inflationary package."

The trouble is that neither economists nor public officials can agree on an explanation—or even on a single collection of explanations. Some analysts argue that the price explosion stems in part from the economic distortions created by wage-price controls, but others are more disturbed by the avoidance of such controls.

Many economists seem to think that most of the problem is explained by poor harvests in the United States and elsewhere and by the Organization of Petroleum Exporting Countries' price increases. Other analysts, such as the University of Chicago's Milton Friedman, think that such special factors don't explain any more than a small part of the latest inflation—and explain none of the underlying problem. There is general agreement that the unusual coincidence of worldwide prosperity in the early 1970s heightened inflationary pressures.

The underlying problem? Some economists think that it is the power of unions to push wages ever higher, while others pin the blame on business pressure for ever-higher prices. But neither theory explains why wages and prices rise much faster at some times than they do at others. An advocate of such theories, says Professor Brunner, must assume that labor or business monopolies now and then decay "with disastrous speed. . . . It is really a remarkable sign of the present intellectual flabbiness that one should seriously discuss such nonsense."

Most analysts do agree that government monetary and fiscal policies have had something to do with inflation both in the United States and abroad. Some economists see the chief sinners as other nations and despair of any real solution until everyone reforms. But others see the United States as the main cause of its own troubles.

Nearly all economists who have bothered to look back a few years agree that the problems have been a long time developing. Specifically they trace much of the trouble to a national attitude epitomized by a 1946 law that Congress passed with the very best of intentions.

In 1946 the United States had just emerged from global war, seemingly in great economic shape. The gross national product in 1945 was $211 billion, more than double the figure for booming 1929. But a lot of that 1945 product was guns, tanks and warships—items no longer in such strong demand. Once the prop of war production was removed, many—if not most —economists saw the United States sagging back into something very much like the depression of the 1930s.

So Congress passed a law. Among other things the Employment Act of 1946 provided that the federal government, with the help of everyone available, should try to promote "maximum employment, production and purchasing power." Most people recognized inflation as an evil but it wasn't the evil of the moment; the act said nothing about it. The overriding aim was to avoid a return to the 1930s.

At the time, that was entirely understandable, but the act set an order of priority that has persisted. "Public policies nowadays," Arthur Burns said in 1974, "are expected to maintain production at a high and rising level, to limit such declines in employment as may occasionally occur, to ease the burden of job loss or illness or retirement, to protect business firms from the hardships of economic displacement, to sustain the incomes of farmers and wage earners, to provide special credit facilities and other assistance to small businesses and home builders and so on."

There had been surges of inflation in earlier years, but each episode was followed within a few years by a general price decline. In the years since World War II, what has gone up hasn't necessarily come down. With minor exceptions in 1949 and 1955, the consumer price index has marched upward each year since the war. The rate of increase began to accelerate in the mid-1960s. Most economists now think that the pace will continue to be swift, at least for several years to come, although the rate of increase had eased by mid-1975. And, of course, the widely feared depression has yet to materialize since World War II.

The overriding interest in output and employment has encouraged the government to spur economic booms by stepping up its own spending and by expanding the supply of money.

When booms have begun to get out of hand and prices have soared, the government usually has moved toward restraint in fiscal and monetary policy. But restraint threatens jobs, so its priority rating in recent years hasn't been the highest.

Moreover, it is difficult to know just when to apply restraint. Economic statistics lag weeks or even months behind the events, and a boom may be out of control before anyone knows it.

High employment and output, furthermore, are so pleasant, and so politically popular, that there is a strong reluctance to rein in the economy before the inflation becomes overpowering.

Several years ago, economist A. W. Phillips produced charts showing that at any given time in any given country a certain rate of inflation was accompanied by a certain rate of unemployment. As a result of this work, some economists and policy makers developed the theory that to get unemployment down it was necessary to accept a higher rate of inflation. Though "a lot" of inflation might be a bad thing, they reasoned, "a little" inflation might be essential.

One trouble with this theory is that the relationship between inflation and unemployment keeps changing—or, as the economists put it, the Phillips curve keeps shifting. In 1973, for instance, the average unemployment rate was 4.9 percent of the labor force while the consumer price index, between December 1972 and December 1973, rose by 8.8 percent. In 1955, by contrast, the unemployment rate was lower—4.4 percent. And consumer prices? They rose by well under 1 percent.

Obviously enough, the economy cannot provide jobs for everyone all the time. Some workers will always be trying to find "better" jobs. Others may lack the skills to qualify for jobs at union wages—or even at government-set minimum wages. Discrimination still is a barrier. At any time a given percentage of the labor force won't find work no matter how energetically the government stimulates the economy with its own spending and easier money.

How large is this percentage? In the early 1960s, government economists guessed that it was around 4 percent, although some of them would have preferred to aim for a lower figure. So the idea was to stimulate the economy until unemployment hit 4 percent and then ease up because additional stimulus would only push up prices.

The labor force, however, continues to change. It now contains relatively more teen-agers and women than it did in 1955, and many of the new workers either are lacking in skills or are only loosely attached to the labor force. Some economists now think that a reasonable minimum goal for unemployment, without inflation, is around 5 percent.

Not everyone agrees with the 5 percent figure. But if it is correct and if policymakers shoot for 4 percent unemployment, they stimulate the economy into more inflation. And that appears to be a large part of the explanation of what has been happening in recent years.

In the past decade or so, a great deal of stimulus has come from the federal budget, with spending mounting every year— and exceeding receipts in every year but one. The Federal Reserve System did its bit to expand demand by stepping up the expansion of the money supply, which is defined as currency plus bank checking accounts.

The money supply, which in earlier years after World War II had grown at a rate of 3 percent or 4 percent a year or so, grew by 6 percent in 1970, by that same figure in 1971, and then by 8 percent in 1972. This is the way the money-supply situation was expressed in a letter to Senator William Proxmire of the Joint Economic Committee by Professor Milton Friedman, a leading advocate of the theory that money is a major influence on the economy:

> "From calendar year 1970 to calendar year 1973, (the money supply) grew at an annual rate of 6 percent; in the preceding decade, from 1960 to 1970, at 4.2 percent. More striking yet, the rate of growth from 1970 to 1973 was higher than for any other three-year period since the end of World War II.

Although economists disagree over the relative importance of fiscal and monetary policy, all agree that such an acceleration of monetary growth portends inflation as the economy begins to run out of things that can be purchased with the expanded money supply. Consumers and businessmen simply bid up the prices of the products and services that are available.

What about the oil price increases and the crop failures? Such special factors cannot produce a general and lasting increase in the price level unless the government helps out by expanding total demand, by increasing the money supply. Otherwise, such factors will only influence relative prices; people will spend more on gasoline and food, less on something else.

Rochester's Professor Brunner would call the oil price increases an institutionalist explanation of inflation. He divides the various explanations of inflations into three groups: the institutionalist, the eclectic, and the price-theoretical.

The institutionalist ideas are perhaps the most evident to the public. They are reflected in such statements as, "The economy doesn't work the way it used to." "Labor unions cause inflation by pushing up wage rates." "Businessmen cause inflation by setting prices wherever they want to."

The oil price cartel, the Organization of Petroleum Exporting

Countries, exerts a monopoly power that would be the envy of any monopolistic-minded businessman. The OPEC countries by no means control all of the world's oil, but they control so much of it that the world could not possibly get along without OPEC supplies for some years to come.

The world's need to buy OPEC oil, moreover, is much stronger than the OPEC countries' need to sell. The OPEC nations know that they hold an exhaustible resource, and most of them would not be reluctant to shut off supplies for a time: The Arab nations' embargo on shipments to the United States was an ample demonstration of that fact.

In general, says Professor Brunner, the institutionalist notions all deny that prices are significantly influenced by the workings of the market, by the interaction of demand and supply. They all contend that price movements emerge from the supply side—from what unions demand as wages, from what businessmen demand as prices.

Such ideas, of course, have been eloquently argued by Harvard economist John Kenneth Galbraith. They are widely accepted by the general public. (Businessmen will believe unions are to blame, while unions are happy to pin the blame on business.)

The wide support for the institutionalist thesis helps to explain why the United States drifted into wage-price control in August 1971. If the root of the trouble was that business or labor or both were making exorbitant demands, the cure was simple: Make it illegal for them to do so.

As Professor Brunner says, though, the institutionalist ideas do not accord with experience. If you're going to blame labor unions, for example, how do you explain periods when prices have declined sharply?

This is not to deny that at certain times and in certain places, labor unions (and business monopolies) may not possess excessive power. They can produce temporary dislocations in wage and price structure, but they do not produce lasting changes in general prices unless government inflates total demand.

In recent years some labor unions have undergone painful demonstrations of this fact. Building trades unions, for instance, pushed up their members' wage rates so much that even a generally inflationary government policy couldn't get them off the hook. Union wages were so high that contractors, whenever possible, opted for nonunion labor. When substitution was not possible many construction projects simply were dropped. What the monopoly power of the building trades unions in the end had accomplished was to price the services of many of their members out of the labor market.

When it comes to institutionalist ideas, "the U.S. government's experiments with controls since August 1971 augmented our evidence in some interesting respects," Professor Brunner says. "Many institutionalist beliefs, and particularly the Galbraithian versions, imply that producers do not respond to price controls with lower supplies, lower qualities, or investment of resources designed to circumvent controls in one way or another. But these reactions have been observed in massive detail in the lumber industry, the food industry and the oil industry whenever controls clashed with market price."

Eclectic ideas about inflation have gained some currency among economists and also among the general public. Some seem to think it's a fine thing to be "eclectic," picking the particular theory that seems to suit the occasion and avoiding any rigid adherence to any particular school of thought.

The eclectic explanations often are combinations of institutionalist ideas or market-oriented theories. The eclectics generally deny that there is any dominant impulse force or pattern in inflation; any particular inflation is caused by whatever happened to cause it. This sort of explanation obviously is of no help to policymakers. The inflation is likely to have proceeded a long way before an eclectic economist can decide what caused it.

Price-theoretical explanations, on the other hand, do at least offer some policy guidance. Professor Brunner enumerates three: the Wicksell-Keynes explanation, the fiscal explanation, and the monetary explanation.

The Wicksell-Keynes explanation, advanced by Sweden's Knut Wicksell and Britain's John Maynard Keynes, argues that "persistent inflations arise from rising entrepreneurial anticipations concerning the real net yield from real capital." In other words, businessmen think they can make more and more money by expanding; this increases private demand. But an unchanged government demand competes for the available resources and inflation results.

Obviously enough, the fiscal explanation centers on government spending: "Inflation is due to a persistent and substantial growth in the government sector's absorption of real resources not released from the private sector by suitable adjustment of tax schedules."

The monetary explanation claims that "inflations as a matter of historical fact are usually produced by monetary influences." An expansion of the money supply, in excess of the growth rate of the economy, is likely to lead to a rise in the general price level.

The monetary explanation, understandably, is the one that monetarist Karl Brunner favors. One trouble with the fiscal and

Wicksell-Keynes explanations is that they do not stand the test of history. In some countries in the past the theories would have indicated that the price developments to be expected would have been quite different from those that materialized.

Even nonmonetarist economists concede that the correlation between monetary trends and price movements is close. But they argue that correlations are not explanations—or at least not fully satisfactory explanations.

Professor Brunner is careful to stress that neither the monetarists nor anyone else has all the answers on inflation: "Our survey does not establish a perfect explainability of inflation in terms of monetary impulses. There remain substantial variation and looseness in the association. But the monetary thesis offers the best explanation of the broad contours of the phenomenon."

The University of Rochester economist also stresses that money is not everything. Changes in real supply and demand can influence relative prices and real phenomena, such as crop failures, can have a broad impact on prices. Fiscal policy is important, not only in the allocation of resources and the distribution of income, but in providing an atmosphere conducive to rational monetary policy.

The Federal Reserve, for instance, will find it far more difficult to control the money supply if it must constantly be making sure that the nation's banks have enough funds to handle a growing flood of Treasury issues.

I . . . offer my opinion that inflation is greatly exaggerated as a social evil. Even while prices are rising year after year, the economy is producing more and more of the goods, services and jobs that meet people's needs. That, after all, is its real purpose.

James Tobin in The New Economics, One Decade Older (*Princeton University Press, 1974*).

chapter 9

Those New Economists

No consideration of how the nation got into the inflationary mess of the early 1970s would be complete without a look at the so-called New Economists who largely shaped government economic policy in the early 1960s. The New Economists were highly critical of the economic policies of the earlier postwar years and were convinced that they could "fine-tune" the economy so that it would do a great deal better.

The Truman and Eisenhower administrations shared the commitments of the Employment Act, the determination to bar a return to the depressed 1930s. But both were also determined to balance the federal budget as often as possible; neither was interested in using fiscal policy to manipulate the economy. Meanwhile the Federal Reserve System of William McChesney Martin fought a sporadic battle against inflation, tightening up whenever it saw a sharp rise in prices.

The result, deplored by the New Economists, was a decade and a half of remarkably stable prices—and several business recessions. None of the recessions even remotely compared with the depression, but they did limit the economy's growth.

It was Richard Nixon's bad luck to be running for president in 1960, just as the last of the series of slumps, all of them officially recognized by the National Bureau of Economic Research, was getting under way. John F. Kennedy campaigned on a slogan, "Let's get this country moving again," and the slogan amid the recession atmosphere proved persuasive.

The newly elected President Kennedy named a Council of Economic Advisers headed by Walter Heller of the University of Minnesota. The council believed that the government, by wise use of financial policies, could promote vigorous and sustainable economic growth. This came to be called the New Economics although it wasn't really new. Economic activism had been tried, with much less than full success, by the Roosevelt administration in the 1930s. Economic activists since the 1930s have said that the chief trouble with the Roosevelt program was that it was too timid, not active enough.

What the New Economists did was to add to the Employment Act commitment a sweeping promise: Not only will we avoid any return to the depressed 1930s but we will do so without even a recession and without inflation. Most important of all, we will keep the economy growing steadily at full-employment levels.

To most Americans, economists or not, it was a little breathtaking. The New Economists proposed nothing less than the abolition of the business cycle, the institution of something very close to perpetual prosperity.

At the start this approach called for new ways of thought. President Kennedy's Council of Economic Advisers stressed the idea of the gross national product gap: the difference between what the economy is producing and what it could produce if all resources were fully employed.

The key resource for this sort of analysis is manpower. The Kennedy economists decided that in the economy of the early 1960s "full employment" was approached when the unemployment rate reached 4 percent of the labor force. There is always a certain amount of joblessness that cannot be eliminated by stimulating the economy with fiscal and monetary policy. Some people are always moving between jobs, looking for better jobs or jobs in better areas. Some people are not fitted for the jobs available in the areas they can or want to reach. At some point, pouring more demand into the economy merely results in bidding up the prices of the available resources; the surplus resources have been used up.

For obvious reasons no one can say exactly where this point is. But the New Economists took 4 percent as their guide; when unemployment fell to that level it was time for the economists to press for steps to ease the inflationary pressures.

The economy that the Kennedy administration inherited was a fine subject for this sort of experiment. It was moving out of the 1960–61 recession only very sluggishly. Industry was operating well below capacity, unemployment still almost 7 percent, and inflationary pressures almost nonexistent.

Some of the Kennedy economists would have preferred to stimulate the economy primarily by stepping up federal spending. They saw what they considered to be many unmet public needs. In the political atmosphere of the time, however, almost any sort of new fiscal stimulus was difficult to achieve. The early moves were modest, such as raising social security benefits without simultaneously increasing social security taxes.

A major limitation on the Kennedy economists was President Kennedy himself. He came to office firmly wedded to the old virtues of fiscal responsibility and budget balance. Added pressure for fiscal rectitude came from the nation's international accounts, which had been out of balance for several years and were causing concern about the world position of the U.S. dollar.

The New Economists have often been referred to as fiscalists, with the strong implication that they think federal spending and taxing policy is all-important. Though they did consider fiscal policy of primary importance, nearly all of them agreed that monetary policy played a major role in the economy. None of them, to be sure, would go as far as the monetarists, such as Milton Friedman, who argued that monetary policy was the dominant influence on short-run economic trends.

Ideally, the New Economists would have liked to have compounded a mix of fiscal and monetary moves to stimulate the economy out of the lethargy of the early 1960s. But there were obstacles. For one thing, monetary moves would be highly visible in world markets and would be likely to have quick impact on the dollar. Moreover, monetary policy was not something that the Kennedy economists could easily influence. William McChesney Martin, the Federal Reserve Board chairman, did not believe that the Fed's performance had been perfect in the 1950s but he by no means shared the New Economists' criticism of it. To Mr. Martin the chief worry was inflation. Even if the international problems of the dollar could be disregarded, it was doubtful that anyone could sell Mr. Martin on a highly expansionary monetary policy.

The New Economists' chief hope was to influence the administration, and even there the going was slow. Mr. Kennedy was elected by the slimmest of margins and, not surprisingly, felt that he should build his political base before embarking on strikingly new initiatives.

Mr. Kennedy had inherited the wage-price guidelines from

the Eisenhower administration. At the beginning the guidelines were supposed to be no more than that—a gentle reminder that when wages rise faster than productivity (output per man-hour) the result is upward pressure on prices. But the Kennedy administration sought to put some muscle in the guidelines, notably in the noisy showdown with U.S. Steel. This episode increased the suspicions of the business and financial community.

In 1962, with the economy still sluggish, there was increased talk of a personal income tax cut. The Kennedy economists would have preferred a temporary cut designed to stimulate demand—an action that could be rescinded if they judged the need for it had passed. But that sort of fiscal tinkering would have been badly received by the financial community, with dangers for the dollar.

The way around this problem, it was decided, was to include a tax cut in a broad overhaul of the tax laws. The cut would not be "temporary" but part of a "reform." Of course putting reform provisions in a tax bill is a good way to guarantee that its progress through Congress will be long and labored. Most of the reforms, such as the moves to end the oil depletion allowance, are aimed at provisions which originally were supposed to insure justice to one group of taxpayers. And each group of taxpayers has its spokesmen in Congress.

Though the reform efforts sagged, the idea of a tax cut steadily picked up support. If you didn't like the idea of the reduction as a device to manipulate the economy, you could view it as a move to let the people spend more of their own money, instead of leaving the spending task to Congress. Conservative publications, such as the *Wall Street Journal*, supported the proposal, as did many business organizations.

President Kennedy didn't live to see the tax cut enacted; it was passed in 1964. By the time it became law, most of the reforms had been stripped away; the cut was on its own.

Even without the tax cut, business had continued to expand. Some would say that is the normal way of the business cycle. The Kennedy economists attributed the uptrend to a largely fortuitous combination of stimulative fiscal and monetary policy. When the tax cut finally was put on the books, whatever economic need there was for it had probably ceased to exist. Although the New Economists did not know it, President Johnson was just about to embark on a massive acceleration of the Vietnam war, which would give the economy all of the stimulus it could contain and then some.

One of the first to point out publicly that the economy was heading into trouble was William McChesney Martin. Then in late 1965 and 1966 the Federal Reserve moved to choke off the growing inflationary pressures by sharply slowing the growth of the money supply. Some of the results weren't pleasant: a severe credit crunch, with a major setback for the housing industry, for instance. But the Fed also did slow the rate of price rise and did it without plunging the country into a real recession—an accomplishment for which the system has received little credit.

It was this action by the Fed, not the New Economists' program, that kept the expansion going. This is not to say that the economists' program was necessarily wrong. If President Johnson had told the economists of the full scope of the Vietnam buildup, they surely would have urged earlier moves to check its inflationary effects. Although there is reason to doubt that the Kennedy economists shared Mr. Martin's view of inflation as the overriding evil, there is no reason at all to doubt that they wanted to prevent severe inflation.

In fact, even without knowing the full scope of the Vietnam expansion, the Council of Economic Advisers urged a tax increase in early 1966. President Johnson rejected the advice, presumably because he feared that Congress would see the need for a tighter fiscal policy as good reason to cut back on the president's domestic social programs.

The investment tax credit was suspended in the fall of 1966, after the Federal Reserve had already curbed the inflationary pressure, and restored in the spring of 1967, after the Fed—alarmed by its success—was once again beginning to stimulate the economy. This and other experiences in the late 1960s highlighted the key problem involved in using fiscal policy to manipulate the economy: Even if economists know exactly what to do and when to do it, Congress or the administration may not be willing to go along.

So the economy continued to heat up, to a point where the overheating became apparent to everyone. President Johnson finally asked for an income tax surcharge, and Congress finally approved it in 1968.

There was great concern among the New Economists and also the members of the Federal Reserve Board that the surcharge would represent inflationary "overkill." Accordingly, the Fed moved to a much easier monetary policy, promoting a more rapid growth of the money supply. To the surprise of many economists, the result was more inflation. Either they had overestimated the impact of the tax surcharge or they had underestimated the potentency of monetary policy.

It was a mixed-up economy that Richard Nixon inherited when he assumed the presidency in 1969. With the surtax in effect, fiscal policy had become less expansionary. The Federal Reserve was becoming conscious of its misreading of the surtax effects and was about to swing to much more restrictive policy. The new Nixon economists proclaimed a program of "gradualism" to get rid of the inflation pressures without pushing the nation into a recession.

Unfortunately, it was not to be. The Fed's restraint in 1969 helped to start the relatively mild recession of 1969–70. This recession became something of a first for the United States: The slump failed to check the inflation. Economists and newspapermen began to talk about stagflation. Previously, inflation and recession had been thought to be incompatible; the country found out that it wasn't necessarily so. The economy began to pull out of the recession in early 1971, but the process was agonizingly slow and prices still continued to rise at rates that, for the time, seemed unacceptably high.

The gross national product, in terms of 1958 dollars, grew rapidly in the first quarter of 1971, but mainly because the economy was bouncing back from the effects of the long auto strike in late 1970. In the second and third quarters the growth rate settled down to a little more than 2 percent, well below the economy's potential. The inflation rate seemed to be slowing somewhat, but opinion polls indicated that the public wanted wage-price controls. The business community made no secret of its desire for controls. At mid-year Federal Reserve Chairman Arthur Burns also called for some form of wage-price restraints.

Although President Nixon repeatedly had voiced his opposition to controls, his administration in August 1971 finally froze prices and freed the dollar to float in international markets. The explanation for the freeze and the subsequent controls was that they were designed to deflate inflationary expectations—while the government checked the inflation with fiscal and monetary restraint.

In the event, however, fiscal and monetary policy before long became highly expansionary. The controls appeared to be effective for a time but gradually began to break down under new inflationary pressures. The controls themselves were progressively eased, except for the interruption of the new freeze in mid-1973, and finally abandoned in May 1974.

The Federal Reserve talked a tough anti-inflation game through this period, but didn't begin to follow through until mid-1974. The administration similarly said all the right things but with lots of help from Congress kept fiscal policy expansionary.

To some extent the Nixon administration was pushed into controls by the New Economists, who had persuaded much of the public that the government could manipulate the economy pretty much as it pleased.

In the Nixon years and the Ford years as well, the New Economists were of course outside critics, not inside participants. Some of them complained, with considerable justification, that newspaper accounts of their ideas had been overblown. Walter Heller, the chairman of President Kennedy's Council of Economic Advisers, had made the mistake of picking up and using what had apparently been a newspaper phrase: fine-tuning of the economy.

The economy is so vast and complex that no group of economists can yet hope to understand all of its working and to be able to prescribe exactly what is the proper federal policy to fit any particular situation. The New Economists themselves know this. But, most of them are firmly convinced that their major problem in the 1960s was not lack of economic expertise but lack of political muscle. James Tobin is not alone in contending that other economists, as well as most politicians, are oversold on the dangers of inflation. Although the words quoted at the beginning of this chapter were written before U.S. inflation soared into double digits, they represent a strong feeling in the economic fraternity that some inflation, and perhaps a good deal of it, must be accepted as the cost of manipulating the economy to ever greater heights of employment and prosperity.

To those who believe that full employment requires inflation, my conviction is that unless inflation is restrained full employment is impossible. I happen to believe that at least relatively full employment on a sustainable basis is not only desirable but feasible and can be achieved with high levels of business activity if we can find some way of containing inflation and maintaining reasonable stability.

William McChesney Martin, former Chairman of the Federal Reserve Board, in Senate testimony in 1973.

chapter **10**

Is inflation essential?

If you're told that you must choose between losing your job and suffering from 10 to 15 percent inflation, you aren't likely to find the choice difficult: Inflation is bad, all right, but *personal* unemployment is surely worse. If the person to lose the job is a stranger who lives across town or, better, in another state, the choice becomes more difficult.

But is such a choice really necessary?

Nearly everyone deplores the fact that some people who want work cannot get it. It is clearly true that the economy furnishes more jobs at a time of strong demand for goods and services than it does at a time when demand is slack. When demand is slack the government can increase it by embarking on expansionary monetary and fiscal policy. So it is that most Americans will go along with heavier government spending and easier money in an economic slowdown.

But that doesn't mean that inflation is essential. The trick is to withdraw the governmental economic stimulants before the patient sets off on an inflationary binge.

That's quite a trick. The stimulants act on the economy only with a lag. By the time the government recognizes that withdrawal is necessary, inflation may be well under way. The early stages of inflation, moreover, can be highly pleasant. There can be and often is political opposition to moves needed to quiet the economy. The upshot sometimes is that the moves come too late.

Even recognizing the proper moment to move is not easy. Economic statistics have been improved immeasurably in recent years, but in many cases they still lag weeks or even months behind the events. Often they are revised later on, frequently in ways that drastically alter the picture of the situation.

The Federal Reserve System, in its control of monetary policy, is not exempt from political pressures but it is less subject to them than Congress. But the Fed does not directly control the money supply. It supplies its member banks with reserves that allow the banks to expand their deposits by making loans.

If the Federal Reserve wanted to slow the rate of growth of the money supply, as it would if inflation appeared to be getting out of hand, it would supply the banks with less reserves. But this move is lacking in precision. For one reason or another it may be weeks before the Fed gets the money supply to act just as it wants. In such delays, the Federal Reserve has been known to become impatient, pushing or pulling harder to get what it wants. As a result it has often gone farther than in wished in one direction or the other.

The tendency toward erratic monetary growth is increased by the fact that the Federal Reserve, in trying to control the money supply, focuses on the interest rate for federal funds, the funds banks lend one another from their excess reserves with the Fed. The Fed predicts what federal funds rate will be consistent with the monetary growth it seeks, and then strives to achieve that rate by putting in reserves or by taking them out. Over the years it has been highly successful in controlling the fed funds rate, but market conditions often change so that it misses its money-growth target.

So heading off inflation is usually a slow and often a rather messy operation. Curbing demand, moreover, is likely to have a highly uneven impact, affecting some areas and some industries more than others. Slower growth of the money supply, at a time when demand for credit is still strong and inflation is heating up, is sure to mean higher interest rates—and troubles for housing, for instance.

When demand is checked that means that businessmen and consumers on the average will be bidding less for the available supply of resources—including manpower. If the supply of resources and their prices were completely flexible, there would be a fairly brief period of readjustment and things would go on much as before.

An auto manufacturer, faced with a reduced demand for cars, could probably sell all he could make if he would cut his price low enough. But if he is to do so, and still earn enough profit to be able to buy new production equipment as his old equipment wears out, he must get his workers and all of his suppliers of parts and materials to agree to reduce their prices too.

His workers, even if no United Auto Workers union existed, would be highly reluctant to cut the prices of their services. Every worker, in the auto industry or any other, becomes accustomed to a certain standard of living. Installment payments are lined up into the future, all of them geared to the maintenance of at least the same income. Wage cuts will be strongly resisted.

In highly organized industries such as autos, unions have

reinforced the resistance to wage cutting. Whatever downward flexibility of wages once existed has been all but eliminated in such industries.

As for the suppliers of parts and materials, they face the same problems as the auto manufacturer. They will find it all but impossible to set their employees to accept wage cuts or to get their suppliers to make price cuts to help out.

One way or another, the auto company has to try to get its costs into line with its revenues. Since the costs of the manpower and materials it uses are not easily flexible downward, the manufacturer takes the alternative: He uses less manpower and materials.

Prices and even wages do go down to some extent—if the deflationary process is long enough and severe enough. But there is not enough flexibility to prevent some significant rise in unemployment.

Since the process of checking demand hits unevenly, the unemployment problem is complicated by the fact that workers cannot or will not move quickly and easily into other jobs that are available. Part of the reason is simply the size and complexity of the economy.

Unemployed ditch diggers in Trenton, New Jersey, may not know that there are lots of jobs for ditch diggers in Palo Alto, California. Even if they do know the jobs are available, they may be financially unable to move to another part of the country. Even if they have the money, they may not want to leave all their families and friends in New Jersey.

In even worse shape are the unemployed ditch diggers who find that the only available jobs call for truck drivers, a job they can't handle. These "frictions" in the job market are always present, but they become a more serious problem at a time when government is trying to check inflation.

The problem has been increased to some unmeasurable extent in recent years by all of the moves to make unemployment less unpleasant. When the auto maker tries to get his costs into line with income by laying off workers, many of those workers continue to draw 95 percent of their normal take-home pay—thanks to unemployment compensation and the supplemental benefits paid by the manufacturers.

Higher jobless benefits generally make it possible for an unemployed worker to wait longer before accepting a job that pays a lower wage or is otherwise less desirable than the job he has lost. This may well be a social gain, but the economic result is that unemployment is probably higher and more prolonged than would otherwise be the case.

The widely publicized unemployment figures provide evidence that whipping inflation now is a costly undertaking. It is costly enough, in any case, that some politicians and economists at some point are likely to decide that some inflation is indeed essential. So the process of reinflating the economy, the job of pumping up demand, begins before the inflation rate has fallen very far. A new boom gets under way, efforts are make to limit it, the same problems arise, the battle is given up, and inflation takes off again from an even higher level.

So is inflation essential?

It may be if you believe that the private economy is inherently unstable, likely to bounce around a lot and leave several million workers without jobs. If you believe that, as many economists do, it becomes necessary for government to be highly active in the economy, constantly either pumping up demand or deflating it, trying to offset the economy's "natural" instability.

Even though, given the political problems, this is not likely to work smoothly and evenly, a wildly erratic private economy can't be left to its own devices. And it may be at least politically essential to accept some inflation rather than the full jolts of the adjustments involved in deflation-inflation cycles.

But the trouble with this is that no one knows whether the private economy is indeed wildly erratic. The University of Chicago's Milton Friedman, among others, argues that the private economy is in fact inherently stable—that the chief source of instability is the government itself.

Otto Eckstein, Harvard economist, member of President Johnson's Council of Economic Advisers and president of the consulting firm of Data Resources Inc., is no disciple of monetarist Friedman. Yet he ran an experiment with an econometric model that indicated to him that the economy would have been better off in recent years if government had stuck to stable monetary and fiscal policies. By "stable" he meant a money supply expanding at a steady and moderate rate and a federal budget that was balanced at full employment.

If the nation should decide to head for such a state—stable government policy—getting there would still involve some pain. Even in a stable economy, one not disrupted by government intervention or anything else, there would be a certain "natural" rate of unemployment. Some people will always be moving between jobs, seeking to better themselves or merely seeking a fresh environment. There will be some problems of adjustment as workers displaced in one location learn about jobs elsewhere or acquire the skills needed elsewhere. Government has a valid and important role in easing these problems of adjustment.

No one knows what this natural rate of unemployment is, but it is probably somewhere near 5 percent. In the process of trying to return the economy to a stable state so that government can stop trying to act as the stabilizer, a return to a normal unemployment rate would be one of the aims. Fiscal policy can and does cushion the unemployment.

What is the inflation aim? Zero inflation is surely unrealistic in terms of any of the existing price indexes. The indexes do not adequately measure quality improvements, so an average rise of around 1 percent a year in the consumer price index is probably the actual equivalent of zero inflation. Since something very close to this was actually achieved during the 1950s and early 1960s, it is not a fanciful goal, outside the realm of possibility.

Once this steady state is achieved—and I do not for a minute want to deny the difficulties of getting there—the government could try to keep itself stable. Keeping the budget balanced at full employment would of course mean actual deficits at times when employment was less than full. (No program is flawless; government would have to guess at full employment, and the actual percentage would have to vary to reflect changes in the character of the labor force.)

A stable fiscal policy does not require any value judgments about the types of expenditures. Spending merely must be adequately covered by revenue, so that the budget will be balanced at periods when the economy is at full employment. As a practical matter, though, such stability will be easier to achieve if the budget is regularly scrutinized to weed out projects that are unneeded or wasteful; the weeding-out leaves room for useful programs within a stable framework.

A stable monetary policy means that the Federal Reserve promotes a steady expansion of the money supply at a moderate rate. What rate? Well, recent experience has indicated that a 4 percent annual rate of growth of "M-2"—currency, bank checking and savings deposits, except for the large certificates of deposit purchased by corporations—would over a period of years be consistent with a price level that rose only slightly.

Promoting a steady rate of monetary growth does not mean

that the Fed would be barred from putting out occasional fires in the money markets. The chances are, though, that market emergencies would be fewer and less severe if government finance itself were stable.

This sort of environment, if it can be achieved, seems to offer greater prospect of promoting long-term high employment than the sort of environment that the nation has lived with in recent years. With stable prices, and with the probability that prices would continue stable, businessmen could plan with more assurance for their future operations. Investments in new plants and machines and in manpower training would look more appealing to private corporations if the future seemed more assured.

Government would still be a major factor in the economy; nothing in this scenario requires government to shrink or even limit future growth. All that is required is that government become a less uncertain factor in the economy, that government operate under certain reasonable rules that everyone knows and understands. When the economy is operating at less than full employment there will be government deficits and the Treasury will be borrowing in the markets. But these usually will be times when private borrowing is reduced.

The present environment, of course, results from efforts to achieve economic stability. The problem is that getting back to stability involves letting the air out of an inflated economy and the experience leaves some people feeling flattened. As a result government in recent years has been inclined to give up the anti-inflation battle before it has been won and set off on a new inflation phase.

The human logic behind such capitulations is that victory against inflation simply costs too many jobs. So we give up and inflate again until the inflation once more becomes too much to bear and we try to curb it again. This is the sort of process the economy has gone through since World War II, with inflation each time taking off from a little higher point.

Over the postwar period the total cost of all of this in jobs lost has been large, and the human suffering has been increased by the fact that the ups and downs of unemployment have been so frequent and so unpredictable. They have been unpredictable in part because businessmen have been unable to plan with assurance in such an environment.

The country has accepted the recurring, continually worsening episodes of inflation because of an assumption that the alternative has been even worse unemployment. It is at least worth asking whether the inflationary instability has not been a major cause of the unemployment problems the nation has had.

The only way that question will ever be answered is by pushing an anti-inflation program through to a successful conclusion. Ideally it should be a broad, carefully organized program that is pressed slowly and gradually.

Such a program cannot be pressed successfully unless most of the public understands what is going on. It cannot be pressed successfully unless government provides intelligent leadership. It cannot be pressed successfully unless government does everything possible to ease the pains of transition to stability.

The alternatives for the United States have long been clear. It can go on the way that it has, stumbling through one inflationary episode after another, accepting frequent surges of unemployment because of a fear of the consequences of the efforts to achieve stability.

Or it can gradually work its way to stability, minimizing the consequences as much as possible. Inflation is not only not essential to a stable, prosperous future; it is totally incompatible with it.

part three

How we may escape

When I came to the Price Commission . . . I expected that after a few months of controls the public would begin to clamor for them to be removed or loosened. The fact is, nearly every public opinion poll shows quite opposite attitudes: More and more people want controls to continue—and many would like them even tighter."

C. Jackson Grayson Jr., Chairman of the Price Commission, in an address to the National Association of Business Economists in September 1972.

chapter **11**
The role of controls

W hen wage-price controls were expiring in the spring of 1974, Cost of Living Council officials, not too surprisingly, thought that the death might be somewhat premature. Speaking to the New York Society of Security Analysts Don R. Conlan, the agency's associate director, said he had gone to Washington with the idea that the market should be allowed to function with a minimum of government interference. Since then, he said, "I have had second thoughts about when or whether the government should stick its hand into the economy."

Although he still thought the market system was best, "there are instances where the free market doesn't work very well." In such instances, he believes, the cost council can get the parties into a room and work out agreements. If the council expires, he asks, "who will address these issues?"

Mr. Conlan put his finger on one of the two major arguments for controls: The free market isn't working very well. Arthur Burns, chairman of the Federal Reserve Board, has said in support of some kind of "incomes policy" that the free market isn't working the way it once did.

John Kenneth Galbraith, the Harvard economist, has argued long and eloquently that the economy essentially is no longer free, that there are large concentrations of business and labor power which effectively control the prices of their products and services. In the public interest, declares Mr. Galbraith, government must set the fees these power brokers charge.

Mr. Galbraith believes that government must take on this responsibility permanently, since he feels that it is politically impossible to take on the power brokers and end their control of prices and wages. Smaller businesses and labor groups can be safely ignored since market forces still do hold down what they charge.

Most other advocates of controls see them only as temporary expedients designed to get us through "emergencies." Until 1971 such emergencies had always been associated with war in one way or another.

When a nation enters a war, particularly on the scale of World War II, massive reallocations of resources and production become necessary. Production of most consumer-type products must be stopped or sharply curtailed, as factories convert to output of war materiel.

The upshot is that the economy booms, generating enormous amounts of income for its workers. But the economy does not produce the quantities of automobiles, appliances, houses, and other items that the workers would like to buy with their expanding incomes. So government is presented with a problem. It can tax away the increases in worker incomes so that the money will not burn holes in the public's pockets. Or it can let the public bid up the prices of available goods, touching off wild inflation. Or it can impose price controls.

In World War II the government more or less accepted a

combination of the three. Taxes were raised, but not enough to siphon off all of the vast increase in incomes. Government felt, probably correctly, that income increases were needed to preserve worker morale and thus to keep the goods flowing to the armed services. Some economists argued, probably also correctly, that more of the war costs should have been financed by taxes to lessen the inflationary pressures that were being built up.

Such arguments found little sympathy in Congress. The University of Chicago's Milton Friedman recalls one such failure in testimony before a congressional committee. What do you need more taxes for, he was asked. "We gave you General Max" (a price control statute).

Price control, however, was not imposed quickly enough or firmly enough to prevent some inflationary price increases, even though controls required an army of more than 300,000, including volunteers. Toward the end of the war, moreover, black and gray markets cast further doubt on arguments that patriotism would make wartime controls effective.

Patriotism did help sell government savings bonds during the war, and bond purchases did help keep inflation in check—until after the war. When the controls were removed the pressures sent prices soaring. I recall being offered, on my return from the navy in 1946, a 1940 Ford for $2,500—more than the car had cost new six years earlier. I decided to walk for a while longer.

Controls again made an appearance during the Korean war, with results that were neither spectacularly good nor spectacularly bad. Thereafter, for much of the next two decades, the United States toyed with various approaches to an incomes policy.

In the beginning the approach was largely academic. President Eisenhower's Council of Economic Advisers pointed out some facts of economic life. For example the council, in its annual report, noted that rising productivity creates a bigger economic pie for everyone.

A simple definition of productivity is output per man-hour. This is relatively easy to measure in manufacturing industries, but very difficult to gauge in the service trades and the professions. No one calls a surgeon highly productive simply because he performs more operations each hour than his contemporaries, for instance.

Nonetheless, rough estimates can be made for most industries and the entire economy. On the average, productivity since World War II has been growing at between 3 percent and 4 percent a year. Thus, the Eisenhower economists advised, wages could rise between 3 percent and 4 percent a year without putting upward pressure on prices.

Some critics objected to this approach, contending that it gave all the benefits of rising productivity to labor. Such critics were merely poor mathematicians, since the increasing productiveness of the economy enlarged everyone's potential share.

Productivity, of course, can grow for many reasons. Up to a point, an increasing average educational level will improve productivity, since it will make workers easier to train. In theory there could be such a thing as an overeducated work force, one that was unwilling to handle many of the repetitive tasks of modern industry.

Good nutrition and health care also can improve productivity. Good management and outside incentives—a popular war, such as World War II—can induce workers actually to work harder. But the chief reason for increased productiveness is still advancing technology and investment in new equipment and production techniques.

If workers demand wage increases that outrun their increases in productivity, however caused, they put pressure on the shares that go to the investors who financed the higher productivity. Management is likely to react by raising prices, or at least trying to.

So the Eisenhower economists simply gave labor and management a little quiet advice. If wage increases were held within the productivity gains, no one would rock the boat and prices would be likely to remain highly stable.

In the early 1960s, President Kennedy's Council of Economic Advisers picked up the advice and converted it into a system of rules. When price or wage increases seemed to the council to be out of line, the parties involved could expect to be summoned by Washington to explain themselves. "Jawboning" more or less became an official government tactic.

All of this seemed to work remarkably well. Until the mid-1960s prices were highly stable; the Consumer Price Index rose at an average of only about 2 percent a year. The major reason for the price stability, though, was that the stop-go fiscal and monetary policy in the Eisenhower years had largely squeezed inflationary expectations out of the economy. In the first half of the 1960s, moreover, there was considerable slack in the economy; it was able to absorb a great deal of economic stimulus without large price effects. The success of the guidelines thus was probably due to market conditions, not to the guidelines themselves.

The fact that wage-price guidelines, accompanied by a little governmental pressure, were not a sure-fire answer for inflation became clear in the mid-1960s. The guidelines collapsed under the demand pressures built up by the expansion of the Vietnam war.

Experience with the guidelines nonetheless shows some of the problems of controls. The basic rule, that wages should not rise faster than productivity, may seem unexceptionable. Yet it leads to all sorts of problems. Partly because productivity for individual firms is hard to assess, efforts were made to set standards for entire industries. Government conceded that productivity would be rising faster for some firms and some industries than others. The answer? Firms with lagging productivity could increase prices, while firms whose productivity exceeded the average could cut prices. The upshot would be, on the average, price stability.

One trouble with that approach is that firms with lagging productivity would probably be the very ones that would have the most difficulty in making price increases stick in the marketplace. Furthermore, firms with increasing productivity very well may be expanding and need to offer extra-high wages to attract the workers they need; price cuts could make such offers impossible.

Tying price increases solely to productivity ignores the role of prices in allocating resources. Growing demand for a product makes it possible for producers to raise prices; the higher prices encourage producers to raise output, and the better balance between demand and supply works to lower prices. When demand for a product weakens, producers and sellers are likely to reduce prices. The lower prices encourage business firms to divert resources to potentially more profitable uses.

The Kennedy-Johnson economists were aware of the problems and therefore sought to administer the guidelines flexibly. But as inflationary pressures grew, the guidelines became less and less effective. Well before President Johnson left office they had been abandoned.

When President Nixon brought back regular wage-price controls in August 1971, the idea was to seek something in between guidelines and the full-dress controls of World War II. Mr. Nixon liked to recall that he had served as a lawyer in the Office of Price Administration in World War II and had been appalled by the red tape and confusion.

The new controls were doomed from the start. Some of the supporters of controls said the problem was the philosophy of the administrators: It was, they said, like putting the Pope in charge of a birth control program. The real problems were more mundane.

Food was an example. Raw agricultural products were exempt from controls. Why? Well, there were several reasons. For one thing, the government was still officially in the business of supporting some farm prices. Federal officials recognized that a strong effort to keep agricultural prices down could depress output (of course, controls could—and did—have a similar effect in other areas).

If that had been the only reason for exempting raw agricultural prices, processed food also would have been exempted. The fact that it wasn't indicated that farmers still have more political power than supermarket chains. With food exempt at one level and controlled at another, the problems of the price controllers obviously were increased. But at least they did avoid the rationing that would have been required by an attempt to control all food.

Controls appeared to work for a time because inflation had been cooling off when the restraints were applied. Controls seem to work when they aren't really needed, when there aren't any strong and growing inflationary pressures to contain. When the pressures grow, as they did a few months after the controls were imposed, the system begins to break down.

The past shows that controls have a role in combatting inflation only in certain highly special circumstances:

1. They are useful when the nation is fighting a major war whose aims are supported by the overwhelming majority of the public, as was the case during World War II. The nation's economy must run full blast, but it must be geared mainly to turn out war materiel, not consumer goods. In such circumstances the public would normally accumulate vast purchasing power but would have little to spend it on.

It is unrealistic to expect any government in such circumstances to siphon off all of this surplus purchasing power through increased taxes. The government could and should have used taxes more than it did in World War II, but taxes could not realistically have done the whole job. In addition to offering savings bonds at attractive rates, the government might have considered some temporary taxes that would have been refunded after the war. But some form of controls was probably unavoidable.

2. It is conceivable that special shocks, such as the quadrupling of oil prices by the Organization of Petroleum Exporting Countries in late 1973, require the government to engage in limited control activity, through allocations or in some other way, in an effort to smooth some of the effects. It is conceivable that the government went too far in the late 1960s and early 1970s in disposing of its agricultural stockpiles, which could have eased some of the effects of bad harvests in the United States and elsewhere. In any case, there can be valid economic emergencies that require governmental intervention on a limited and temporary basis.

3. There is a case, though not a strong one, for a temporary wage-price freeze while the government implements true anti-inflationary policies: restraint in federal spending and in monetary expansion. Such a case could exist if government had been steadily building up the inflationary pressures and had at long last decided to mend its ways. A freeze could help to provide breathing room for a brief period. This was of course one of the arguments used for the August 1971 freeze, although the facts did not fit the argument. More often than not, as in August 1971, controls are used to try to head off the effects of increasingly inflationary policies.

4. The final case for controls is entirely political. It exists if government is unwilling or unable to keep its own spending programs within the limits of the resources that it is willing to tax away from the private sector. It exists if government is unwilling or unable to face up to any excessive concentrations of power in labor or business. It exists if government permits the supply of money regularly to grow faster than the supply of goods the money will buy.

It exists, too, if government persists in granting special favors to special-interest groups. One such favor was the Davis-Bacon Act, which in effect requires government contractors to pay prevailing union wages, whether they employ union workers or not. President Nixon at one point suspended the act, but he restored it when the construction unions—the chief unions affected—agreed to go along with a voluntary program aimed at restraining wage increases.

Davis-Bacon is only one example of far too many. The law requires that some government-financed cargoes be carried in U.S. ships, even though costs are higher. Congress in 1974 passed a bill to require that part of U.S. oil imports be carried in U.S. tankers. Regulatory agencies, supposedly set up to protect the public interest, often wind up protecting their industries from competition; the Interstate Commerce Commission, for instance, shields trucks and water carriers from railroad rate cuts.

If government permits all of these things to happen, it may have something of an obligation to try to smother the effects with controls. The effort won't work; in all probability, the government then would see its only choice to be even tighter controls. The existence of fully socialized states such as the USSR shows that it is possible to have a viable economy under full central management, but that is not an option that many Americans willingly would elect.

The central strength of the American economy up to now has been its large measure of freedom. Resources move freely from one use to another that promises to be more productive. The movement is induced and rewarded by a system of free prices and wages. The free market is not a perfect system; it is merely the best yet found.

The government has a difficult role in promoting the freest possible economy—and in helping those who suffer unfairly from its workings. Government quickly creates trouble for itself, as well as for much of the public, when it tries to reshape the free economy to produce better results for everyone. The long effort to manage the farm economy is a prime example. The alleged reason for the effort was to protect the small and poor farmers; in practice, most of the benefits have gone to the large commercial farms.

In sum, controls have no valid role in a long-run battle against inflation. Realistically, their use should be limited to major wars and perhaps periods when there have been temporary and severe economic shocks.

In short, the Fed should cease warping a sound monetary policy in order to compensate for what it considers to be the frailities and shortcomings of the rest of government. Far better, let the Fed pursue a sensible monetary policy, and provide a profile in courage by telling the rest of government and the public the measures that are needed to get on the track of maximum employment, maximum productivity and maximum purchasing power.

Representative Henry S. Reuss (D., Wis.) in a statement to the House Banking and Currency Committee, April 4, 1974.

chapter 12
The role of the Fed

The founders of the Federal Reserve System never saw the primary task of their creation as the promotion of stable prices. The Fed grew out of a realization that the existing "dual" banking system, composed of state and national banks, was dangerously unstable. Recurring panics had driven the point home, and the severe disturbance in 1907 finally pushed the Congress into action.

A major trouble with the existing setup was that banks kept their reserves with other banks; if one bank failed, it was likely to pull down a succession of others. Moreover, funds did not flow easily from one part of the country to another; banks in one area could have excess funds while banks in another area were strapped.

The Reserve System was supposed to hold the reserves of most major banks and through loans and in other ways make credit reasonably accessible in all parts of the country. Americans of the early 20th century still distrusted the notion of one central bank, so the System was set up as 12 regional banks, with a coordinating board in Washington.

From the beginning in 1913 there was confusion. Individual Reserve Banks sometimes pursued individual monetary policies that were opposed to one another. The Federal Open Market Committee finally evolved as System officials recognized the need to coordinate activities. The committee now is composed of the 7 members of the Reserve Board, the president of the New York Reserve Bank, and 4 of the other 11 Reserve Bank presidents, serving on a rotating basis.

The New York bank president has a permanent seat on the committee because the bank, located in the nation's financial capital, has always been the system's most important. Through the early years of the system's history, in fact, the president of the New York bank was the dominant official of the Federal Reserve.

Even with coordination, the system has been slow in learning its role. During the period from 1929 to 1933 the Fed let the nation's supply of money, consisting of currency and bank checking accounts, shrink by more than one third, a development that had more than a little to do with the depth of the economy's decline.

During and after World War II the Federal Reserve was involved in helping the Treasury finance its massive rise in debt. The Fed's actions first and foremost were directed at keeping down the interest costs of the Treasury securities by supporting the securities' prices in the market. Finally, in 1951, an agreement between the Treasury and the Fed released the system from this price-support responsibility.

After the Treasury-Fed accord, William McChesney Martin, Jr., who had been a Treasury official, became Federal Reserve chairman, and some cynics suspected that the Fed's new freedom was more apparent than real.

In 19 years at the demanding job, however, Mr. Martin led the Federal Reserve to a deeper appreciation of its responsibilities. From the vantage point of the inflated 1970s, especially, the 19 Martin years look like an oasis of stability.

Mr. Martin is no economist, and when he retired in 1970 many economists were pleased to see Arthur F. Burns, a veteran of Columbia University and the National Bureau of Economic Research, move into the job. His friend Milton Friedman, the University of Chicago monetarist, hailed Mr. Burns as the right man in the right place at the right time. Before many months went by he began to wonder about that assessment.

In the first 4 years of Mr. Burns's chairmanship, the Federal Reserve allowed the money supply to grow at an annual rate of about 7 percent, well above the average growth rate of the 1960s. Mr. Burns was not inclined to accept the blame for the resulting inflation; he stressed the price increases by the Organization of Petroleum Exporting Countries, loose fiscal policy, worldwide crop failures, and assorted other factors. In 1971 he was an early advocate of some form of price control.

Frequently, the chairman pleaded for help in battling inflation but little or none was forthcoming. Finally, in mid-1974, the Fed apparently gave up and decided to go it alone, tightening money sharply.

The Federal Reserve influences the money supply chiefly by buying and selling Treasury securities in the open market. A vice president of the New York Reserve Bank handles the system's open market account, operating in a trading room at the New York bank—a fact that partly explains the continuing importance of the New York Fed.

Member banks of the Federal Reserve System are required to keep deposits at their regional Reserve Banks; these deposits, plus cash in their vaults, make up their reserves, which must equal a specified percentage of the deposits on the member banks' own books.

When the Fed buys Treasury securities from a member bank, it pays for them by crediting the reserve account of the member bank. When the Federal Reserve buys from a nonbank, such as an industrial corporation, the process is somewhat more complex but the result is the same. The seller is paid with a Federal Reserve check, he deposits the check in his bank, the bank sends the check to the Fed, and the Fed credits the bank's reserve account.

When a member bank acquires more reserves it can expand its deposits and usually does so, chiefly by making loans. As deposits rise, so does the money supply.

Even this brief recital should show that there is no way to be sure of expanding the money supply—or shrinking it—by precise amounts within specified periods. Until recent years, in fact, precise control of the money supply has not been a primary Federal Reserve aim.

The primary aim was to promote something called stable money market conditions. Freely translated, this meant that the Fed tried to prevent what it considered to be undue fluctuations in interest rates. At times this effort could be in accord with promoting stable prices; at times, it might not be.

When interest rates rose, the Federal Reserve tended to assume that money was tight; stabilizing the money market thus required an injection of additional funds. But interest rates, as businessmen lately have learned, can reflect more than the supply of and the demand for credit.

They can reflect inflation. When lenders expect more inflation they insist on higher interest rates to try to offset the decreasing value of the dollar. Borrowers, of course, are willing to pay the higher rates because they know they can repay the loans in cheaper dollars. In such a circumstance, a Federal Reserve attempt to get interest rates down by pumping more funds into the economy is likely only to push rates higher by increasing inflationary expectations.

Since 1972 the Fed has begun to pay more attention to the monetary aggregates, such as the money supply. The narrowly defined money supply, currency and bank checking accounts, is known as M-1. A broader definition, wrapping in bank time deposits (except for large certificates of deposit sold to corporations), is known as M-2.

But interest rates remain important. The chief rate the Federal Reserve watches is the rate for so-called federal funds, the excess reserves that member banks lend to one another for very short periods of time. The Open Market Committee sets targets for the monetary aggregates and then decides what sort of a fed funds rate is "consistent" with that target.

This approach has attractions of convenience. The fed funds rate is constantly available to the New York trading desk as it seeks to carry out the directions of the Open Market Committee. Moreover, the Fed can count on being able to influence the funds rate quickly and even fairly precisely on a short-term basis. When the Federal Reserve puts reserves into the banking system, it increases the potential supply in the funds market and tends to depress the funds rate.

Money supply statistics are harder to come by and less reliable, in part because the Reserve System paid so little attention to the money stock until lately. The figures are available on a weekly basis but they are usually subject to later revision, and some of the changes can be drastic.

No one argues, however, that federal funds rates themselves have much effect on the economy. On the other hand, nearly everyone now agrees that changes in the rate of growth of the money supply are a major, if not the dominant, influence on short-run business trends. There are still sharp disputes among economists; some analysts, for instance, argue that the Federal Reserve expands or contracts the money supply only in response to developments in the economy and, realistically, has no choice in the matter.

Over a period of three months or so, however, nearly everyone now agrees that the Fed can control the money supply with a high degree of precision. "In the short run it's a question of ability," James L. Pierce, associate director of the Reserve Board's Division of Research and Statistics, said at one point. "In the long run it's a question of willingness."

There is no perfect monetary target. In late 1974, for example, the Federal Reserve was trying to push down the federal funds rate, since a lower rate seemed consistent with somewhat more rapid expansion of the money supply. But the rate, which had fallen from over 12 percent to less than 9 percent in a few months, for a time seemed to resist the pushing. One reason apparently was that banks outside New York had become less interested in the market as the rate fell and were trying harder to find uses for excess reserves in their own areas.

Some economists argue that the Federal Reserve should watch something called the monetary base, composed of currency in circulation and the reserves of member banks. Reliable estimates of the base can be obtained much more easily and often than estimates of the money supply, and the bulk of the base—the reserves—is directly controlled by the Fed.

Even this approach is not completely reliable. Over time there has usually been a predictable relationship between the monetary base and the money supply. In the last half of 1974, however, an unusual public demand for currency distorted this relationship, so that the money supply did not grow nearly as fast as the base.

Since the banks hold fractional reserves, an additional $1 in reserves permits a much greater rise in deposits—and the money supply. An additional $1 in currency does not have the same multiplier effect. Of all the available alternatives, though, the monetary base seems the best.

In any case, when the Federal Reserve decided to crack down on inflation in mid-1974, no arguments over technique stopped the action. In the summer and early fall, the money supply grew at an annual rate of around 2 percent. Minutes of the Open Market Committee meetings, released several weeks after such gatherings, show that the crackdown was somewhat more severe than the committee had intended. But the error apparently was of degree, and definitely not of direction.

The tightening was so severe that the Shadow Open Market Committee, a group of uninvited advisers to the real committee, found itself calling in September 1974 for somewhat swifter monetary expansion. The shadow group, composed of monetarists such as the University of Rochester's Karl Brunner, had previously been deploring excessive monetary growth.

For once, the real Open Market Committee appeared to agree with the shadow group. At President Ford's economic summit in September, Chairman Burns sought to reassure everyone. He didn't specifically say that the Federal Reserve was easing up, and he did reaffirm the system's determination to persevere in the fight against inflation. But he also said that the Fed would see to it that the supply of money and credit continues to expand. "There will be no credit crunch in this country," he said.

Well, there are credit crunches and credit crunches, and many businessmen in late 1974 thought they already had one. But there was no question that the Federal Reserve was easing up, trying to do so very gradually, a trick that it has always found difficult to master.

The fact that even monetarists concede that the Federal Reserve cannot precisely control the money supply over a short period of time helps increase doubts about using monetary policy to try to "fine-tune" the economy. When inflation is rampant, as it was in late 1974, the Fed has little choice but to slow the growth of the money supply. But if the economy ever gets back to stability, the first role of the Federal Reserve will be to stabilize itself.

The chief reason that monetary policy has been so destabilizing in the past has been that it has been so changeable. The Fed has usually moved too late and gone too far.

Monetarists urge that the Federal Reserve seek to expand the money supply at a constant, moderate rate. This does not mean that the Fed would be foreclosed from dealing with financial emergencies. The system must be a lender of last resort, a defense against financial panics. But this does not oblige the Federal Reserve to keep every bank from failing; it merely obliges the Fed to keep the failure from spreading to solvent banks and institutions. If the Fed gets involved in trying to rescue each and every company and industry that gets in trouble, responsible monetary policy becomes impossible.

A constant, steady rate or monetary expansion, moreover, means a rate that is averaged over a period of at least a quarter. The Federal Reserve probably could hit such a target more accurately if it paid less attention to the level of interest rates. For that matter, a stable monetary policy would tend to produce a more stable interest rate pattern.

As some Federal Reserve officials long have contended, the execution of monetary policy is too important for the Fed to be burdened with all of the financial housekeeping chores that have been handed to it by Congress. The Federal Reserve, for instance, is deeply involved in the messy arrangements for Federal supervision of banks.

The Comptroller of the Currency in theory regulates all nationally chartered banks, the Federal Deposit Insurance Corporation regulates insured institutions, and the Federal Reserve regulates its members. Supposedly the agencies have worked out ways to minimize the overlaps, but one federal regulator—not the Fed—seems a much better idea.

What rate of monetary expansion is proper? The question is secondary; stability of the rate is of primary importance. But the growth rate should be large enough to accommodate the normal growth of the economy and, it would be hoped, a decreasing amount of inflation. As we said earlier, zero inflation, in terms of existing price indexes, is probably impossible. Advancing technology makes quality improvements that the indexes cannot catch.

Stable expansion of the money supply at a modest rate naturally assumes that the private economy is inherently stable. That's a large assumption. But it is clear that monetary policy in recent years has increased instability, and it would be interesting to see what the economy could achieve with such "help."

During past fiscal years of very large budget deficits, the Treasury has been involved in some sort of financing the majority of the time, which has left the monetary authorities little opportunity to unwind.

Darryl R. Francis, President of the Federal Reserve Bank of St. Louis, in his bank's June 1974 Review.

chapter 13
The role of the budget

If monetary policy has been unstable since World War II, fiscal policy has been wildly erratic. About the only element of consistency is that the government in nearly every year has spent more money than it has taken in as tax receipts.

Franklin Delano Roosevelt campaigned for the presidency in 1932 in part on a promise to balance the federal budget. Such a promise was bad economics amid the depression, and it was even worse economics when the Roosevelt administration raised taxes sharply to try to keep the promise.

Yet Republican politicians in later years continued to campaign against the fiscal irresponsibility of the Democrats. So when a Republican returned to the White House in 1953, Dwight Eisenhower proceeded to achieve a record peacetime deficit—the $12 billion of 1958.

Lyndon Johnson broke that record with the combination of spending on the Vietnam war and the Great Society social programs at home. But Richard Nixon, another supposedly fiscally responsible Republican, set new highs in fiscal years 1970 and 1971.

Of course it's unfair to tag any president with the full blame for what happens to the federal budget while he is in office. Even Franklin Roosevelt, with solidly Democratic Congresses, didn't always get exactly what he wanted from the lawmakers. When Gerald Ford came to office after the Nixon resignation, he urged spending cuts as anti-inflation steps and got little help from Congress. The fact is that both presidents and Congresses, of both major parties, have long since ceased to pay much attention to the "old-time religion" of balanced federal budgets.

Just how valid was that old-time religion? As I have already suggested, it didn't make sense for the government to try to balance the budget amid the depression. The effort was inherently self-defeating. The government sharply increased its tax rates, taxing away income that corporations and individuals otherwise might have invested toward the production of additional taxable income.

If the economy is operating well below its capacity, as it certainly was during the mid-1930s, nearly all economists now agree that government deficits are desirable and pose no inflation danger. Even if the economy is running at full capacity, a government deficit is not necessarily inflationary.

When the government spends more than it takes in, it obviously has to find the money somewhere. In other countries and at other times, governments have solved the problem simply by printing more paper money. The U.S. approach is more sophisticated: When outgo exceeds income, the Treasury borrows the difference.

If the Treasury borrows the money from you and me, the impact is not inflationary. All that happens is that you and I have less money to spend and the Treasury has more.

Of course some of us will question whether the government

should spend our money. There may be reason to wonder, too, whether public spending always contributes as much to productivity as private spending does. However that may be, the direct and immediate impact of the shift in the spending pattern will not be inflationary.

In the real world, though, a large share of the new Treasury securities wind up in the Federal Reserve Banks. The Fed now owns more than $80 billion of federal securities, an increase of well over 60 percent in the last seven years. The Federal Reserve buys the securities in the market, and when it does it increases the commercial banks' reserves—and thus the banks' ability to expand loans, deposits, and the money supply.

Darryl R. Francis, president of the St. Louis Federal Reserve Bank, discussed this process in the bank's *Review*. "In the decade 1952 until the latter part of 1961," he said, "the net government debt rose by a total of about $22 billion. Of that amount, the Federal Reserve System, through its open market operations, purchased and therefore monetized about $5 billion."

As a result the money supply—and prices—rose only slowly during the 1950s and into the 1960s.

From late 1961 to late 1970, by contrast, net government debt expanded by $48 billion and Federal Reserve holdings grew by $33 billion. In the following three years, net debt grew by $49 billion and the Fed purchased over $17 billion.

Perhaps Federal Reserve operations would have been inflationary even without the huge rise in federal debt. But the Treasury borrowing creates serious problems for monetary policy.

The Federal Reserve is and long has been concerned with the level and trend of market interest rates. When the Treasury comes to market with a new securities offering, it competes with private borrowers and, all other things being equal, puts upward pressure on rates.

"During periods when deficits are large," says Mr. Francis, "upward pressure on market interest rates—downward pressure on securities prices—occurs at the time the Treasury financings take place. In the past the Federal Reserve often has 'even-keeled' the money market—that is, provided reserves through open market operations to 'lean against' the tendency for interest rates to rise in the short run."

> In theory, the Federal Reserve would "unwind" after the even-keel operation by reducing its portfolio of securities. In practice, the desire to resist upward pressure on market interest rates, especially during periods of a strengthening economy and rising demands for credit, has militated against behaving according to this ideal.
>
> Also, during past fiscal years of very large budget deficits, the Treasury has been involved in some sort of financing the majority of the time, which has left the monetary authorities little opportunity to unwind.

In theory the Federal Reserve does not have to get so wrapped up in overseeing Treasury financing operations. In practice there is little else the Fed can do. If the system began to allow Treasury borrowings to fail, Congress soon would take a hard look at the Fed's cherished independence.

As a practical matter, the Federal Reserve cannot refuse to monetize a large portion of the big federal deficits. So any program to check inflation must include an effort to hold down those deficits. And any program to achieve lasting stability must include an effort to avoid those wide swings in federal budget policy.

Richard Nixon correctly stated the problem in his 1974 *Eco-*

nomic Report. The nation has learned several lessons in its past efforts to check inflation, he said. High among them was "a need for a greater steadiness of policy."

> Sharply squeezing down the economy in an effort to halt inflation [he continued] would produce a sharp drop in employment and economic activity and create demands for a major reversal in policy. Pumping up the economy to get quickly to full employment would risk setting off even swifter inflation.

How true. It could be added that abrupt changes in policy, as well as fears of such changes, can greatly increase economic uncertainty. When businessmen and consumers plan their spending, they like to think they have some idea of what will happen next. If they don't, their spending—or nonspending—can send the economy into strange gyrations.

Having stated the problem, Mr. Nixon implicitly pointed up the difficulties governments find in solving it.

The economy had begun to slow down after the booming first quarter of 1973, and the Nixon administration had accepted the idea that some slowing was both inevitable and desirable to avoid runaway inflation. However, Mr. Nixon said in his budget message for fiscal 1975, "This slowdown should not be permitted to go too far."

Of course not. But how do we keep the slowdown from going "too far"? Well, said the president, "I propose a budget that will continue a posture of moderate restraint rather than greatly intensifying that restraint. Also, my administration is developing and will be prepared to use a range of measures to support the economy if that should be necessary."

The questions keep coming up. How does the administration decide that the slowdown has gone "too far"? How will it know the moment when it is "necessary" to support the economy?

The answer is simply that there isn't any answer—at least, no specific one. Economic analysis is still so uncertain that it's often difficult to get agreement as to where the economy has been recently, let alone where it is now or is likely to be in the near future.

In his State of the Union message in 1974, Mr. Nixon firmly promised that there would be no recession, and George Shultz, then Secretary of the Treasury, was later asked what a recession is. Mr. Shultz noted the simple definition often cited in the press: two consecutive quarters of decline in the gross national product, stated in constant-value dollars. But the simple definition, he emphasized, didn't fit the early-1974 situation, complicated as it was by energy problems.

What definition did fit? In a good-humored way the secretary avoided any real reply. The administration, he said, would try to screen out the short-term effects of the energy crisis in deciding whether we had a real recession on our hands.

In other words, the layoffs caused by Detroit's efforts to shift from big-car to small-car production were not evidence of recession. But production cutbacks and layoffs caused by a fall in demand for cars of any kind would be evidence of recession.

Of course a recession does not have to be official to require government action, Mr. Shultz said. By that time, he remarked, it may be too late to do anything about it. With a smile he noted that the private National Bureau of Economic Research, which keeps careful watch on business cycles, will probably let us all know "two and a half years from now" whether or not we've had a recession. (Actually the bureau decided before the end of 1974 that a recession did indeed exist.)

So the government doesn't wait for an official recession. In

Mr. Nixon's *Economic Report* he said that "in this unpredictable economic environment" we're going to need "alertness and adaptability." To put it another way, we can't predict what's going to happen but we're going to have to stay on our toes and try to predict it anyway.

The administration, said Secretary Shultz, had a range of ideas about what to do if the economy appeared to sag too much, however much that might be. He noted that the government had innumerable projects that could be speeded up or slowed down as the need was indicated.

But the nagging question kept recurring. How does the administration decide it must act? The secretary said the best way was simply to keep monitoring the economy the way we always have. If the administration decided that there had been too much change in economic conditions it would simply propose changes in federal programs.

In retrospect, of course, we know now that the administration for a variety of reasons was not able to prevent the slump from developing into a full-fledged recession. An important reason was the Federal Reserve's switch to tough monetary restraint in mid-1974.

The involvement in Watergate obviously complicated matters in 1974. But even without that, is it reasonable to expect that any administration will know just when and how to move?

In the past few years we have learned a great deal about the economy, but the statistics still remain incomplete and imperfect, as well as weeks or months late. Figures on vital segments of the economy must regularly be revised. Can we be sure that an action taken on the strength of the preliminary figures will not seem unwise when the final statistics arrive?

Even if the figures were perfect, no one yet knows exactly

how and when changes in fiscal and monetary policy will affect the economy. And even if we did know, there remain all of the complications of the political process. The administration could propose the wisest possible fiscal move and Congress might debate it for so long that by the time it was enacted it would be exactly the wrong move.

Every new federal spending program quickly builds up its own constituency and becomes difficult to change or eliminate. Whatever its influence on the economy, changing the federal budget is a clumsy way to maneuver.

Fortunately, however, the federal budget has a certain built-in flexibility. In a boom, federal tax receipts go up with everything else and—if new spending programs are avoided—the budget tends to move toward balance. In a recession federal tax receipts fall and spending on unemployment compensation, welfare, and other social programs rises, tending to push the budget away from balance.

Building on this flexibility it has become fashionable in recent years to talk of something called the "full-employment budget." This is an entirely theoretical concept: what the budget would look like if the economy were operating at full capacity. If it is carefully handled, however, the concept has its virtues.

In the first place, the idea calls for some assumptions about full capacity. In his final budget, for instance, Richard Nixon was still assuming that full employment meant an unemployment rate of 4 percent of the labor force. Many economists now believe that full employment is closer to 5 percent, since the labor force now includes many teen-agers and women who are less firmly attached to the force than many workers.

If you assume the budget should be balanced at full employment, and you think that 4 percent is full employment, you build a budget with an actual deficit that is larger than you would have if you think 5 percent is "full." A larger deficit means more problems for the Federal Reserve in handling the resulting Treasury financing—and more inflation dangers. The Treasury, after all, has to worry about actual deficits, whatever the full employment budget may say.

If the concept is handled carefully, though, it may help in explaining that actual budgets at some times should be in surplus (yes, surplus), at some times in balance, at some times in deficit. And it should reach those positions in large part automatically.

That doesn't mean that certain spending programs should not be changed from time to time and others started or canceled. The entire budget needs more regular and more searching scrutiny than it has been getting.

The budget is a key tool for allocating the nation's resources, particularly over a long period of time. Congress has a continuing responsibility to screen out programs that are no longer serving the purposes for which they were intended. It needs to consider the budget more as a complete document and less as a miscellaneous collection of spending programs, and perhaps its new budget committees will make this possible.

At best the budget is not an effective weapon in coping with short-term economic trends. At worst it can vastly complicate the job of the Federal Reserve.

The real causes of inflation lie deeper than
monetary factors. They nonetheless are not
unalterable. The present widespread concern
about inflation gives hope that people will
indeed demand changes in economic structure
and policy that will bring down inflation."
*Henry Wallich, Member of the Federal Reserve
Board, in a speech on July 18, 1974.*

chapter **14**
Changing the structure

One argument for wage-price controls has always been that the economy simply isn't working as it should. Sure, the government can curb inflationary pressures by slowing the growth of the money supply and curbing its own spending, but the results are likely to include some unpleasant shocks, such as a rise in unemployment. Controls are supposed to permit the government to soften the financial restraint, applying it over a longer period. The inflated demand will be gradually squeezed out of the economy but the controls will slow wage-price increases right away.

In the past the technique hasn't worked very well. Politicians often see the controls as an excuse for shunning any financial restraint. In any case, the controls in time distort the economy, foster black markets, and waste scarce resources.

Against that background it seems sad that more effort has not been made to eliminate excuses for controls by making the economy operate more efficiently, more competitively. Clearing out some of the anticompetitive underbrush—changing the structure—would do more than make the response to monetary-fiscal restraint less painful. It would reduce the number of occasions when such restraint is needed.

Government in 1973 and 1974 took a few steps in the right direction. The swift rise of farm prices swept away much of the farm price-support program. After literally years of delay, Congress in late 1974 finally voted a bill that will permit the administration to negotiate further liberalization of international trade.

Yet such gains may be illusory. At about the time the trade bill was passed the Ford administration, under prodding from cattlemen, announced that it would try to get other nations to limit "voluntarily" their meat exports to the United States—and thus in one step managed to raise doubt both about farm market freedom and the U.S. commitment to freer trade.

The importance of freer trade to checking inflation is self-evident. Markets are broadened, putting pressure on U.S. producers to increase their own efficiency. Since the government put up the barriers against free trade, it has an obligation to ease the problems attendant on the barriers' removal. Through worker retraining and other ways it can help the transfer of resources to more economic uses.

The alternative is to wall off the noneconomic company or industry from the world with tariffs or quotas, enabling it to charge higher prices. Though such protection is usually called temporary, there is nothing in the setup that promises the protected industry will ever become economically viable. So consumers are likely to go on subsidizing inefficiency through high prices.

That surely is an unappealing alternative for the public in a period of high inflation. But early in 1975 export market competition was heating up and countries tried to earn funds to pay for more expensive oil. A new flood of imports into the United States could darken the chances for new progress toward freer trade.

Organized labor, long a friend of free trade, has swung the other way in recent years. Union officials argue that imports are costing their members jobs. Unions also have inveighed against U.S. companies with subsidiaries overseas, arguing that such companies were exporting jobs. High levels of unemployment could lend credence to such charges—and endanger any trade talks.

Labor unions also loom large in another area where reforms are needed: wage costs. One reason that unemployment seems to rise almost automatically as monetary-fiscal restraint checks inflation is that unions have helped to make wages really flexible only in an upward direction.

When a businessman faces a decrease in demand, he naturally tries to reduce his costs. In most cases, the only way that he can cut his labor costs quickly is by laying off workers.

Forty years ago labor unions were economic underdogs, so the government moved to put them on equal terms with management. The move simply went too far. In 1947 and 1959 Congress became concerned enough about unions' abuse of their power that it passed restraining laws: the Taft-Hartley Act and the Landrum-Griffin Act.

More recently, many people appear to have decided that the only possible response to union power is controls. Management supported Richard Nixon's first price freeze in August 1971 largely because it saw no other way to stop the upward sweep of wage costs.

"Management seems to be increasingly doubtful that it can win major strikes," said Henry Wallich, member of the Federal

Reserve Board, in a July 1974 speech. "Unions seem increasingly confident of their strength."

> Political factors, the economic damage from major strikes, unemployment compensation for strikers in some states, the expectation of both management and labor that the effect of high wage increases will be compensated by expansive public policies—all favor strong demands by labor and their acceptance by management.

What to do about labor? Well, the most important measure is simply to check the inflation itself. Labor unions are ponderous political organizations. Two- and three-year or even longer contracts have suited their convenience as well as management's desire for stability. By the time unions come to the bargaining table for a new contract, they may feel with some justification that inflation has wiped out a lot of the gains they made the last time around.

Union officials, moreover, simply cannot afford to assume that some such development will not follow any new contract they negotiate; if they do, they may lose their jobs at the next union convention. If anything, the officials may try to overcompensate for the inflation they expect.

Even a return to reasonably stable prices, however, would not guarantee that all unions would always be reasonable in their demands, or that all managements would be reasonable in their response.

Making any significant change in the situation will be difficult indeed, and not only because of union political opposition. One approach often suggested is to move to compulsory arbitration. But arbitrators too often are inclined to split the difference between the parties, even if one side may be 100 percent right. As a result there is no guarantee at all of labor peace.

One variant of arbitration that has been proposed is to press bargaining until it is apparent no agreement can be reached. Then each side would present its final position and a government arbitrator would choose between the two positions.

The arbitrator could not pick out parts of one position and meld them with parts of the other; it would be an either-or proposition. The idea has obvious virtues. Both sides would be inclined to leave clearly unreasonable points out of their final position, since they would increase the chances that the arbitrator would simply vote for the other side.

Whatever is done, it clearly is time for a thorough look at labor law.

Minimum wage laws were enacted by federal and state governments with only the very best of intentions. When the minimums remain well below average wages and jobs are relatively plentiful, the pay floors may do little harm and may actually curb some employers from exploiting their workers.

But labor unions have helped to keep the minimums constantly moving higher, and jobs sometimes are less than plentiful. The result has been that minimum wages sometimes can make it difficult for young and inexperienced workers to get any jobs at all. At the least the laws should be revised to provide some downward flexibility for youthful workers.

Labor unions also make it difficult for the young and inexperienced to enter the labor force by setting high starting wages. Companies no longer find it economic to hire the unskilled and train them on the job.

For a half-century the federal government has been trying to keep labor peace on the nation's railroads. The result has been to so enhance the power of the multiplicity of craft unions that railroad costs have often been pushed to prohibitive levels.

Consider a 1972 strike against the Long Island Railroad, which normally carries 90,000 commuters to and from New York City every day. The Long Island had become so unprofitable that it finally was taken over by a governmental agency. But governmental operation, like governmental regulation, has not produced labor peace.

In the strike 12 unions, representing 5,000 carmen, teamsters, clerks, electrical workers, sheet metal workers, and other nonoperating employees, as well as some supervisors, rejected the pay proposal of a federal emergency board. The trouble with the proposal was that it called for a smaller increase than the one granted earlier to operating employees. Interunion bickering has always been a major cause of rail labor strife.

The operating unions got their larger increase as a sort of bribe to induce them to give up costly and archaic work rules. But this did not lessen the nonoperating unions' desire for "parity."

Bigger increases for the strikers naturally would have to be absorbed by the public. Meanwhile, the strikers lined up for unemployment benefits. This situation resulted from the fact that railroad workers after the fourth day of a legal strike qualify for benefits from the Railroad Retirement Board.

No one wants to see anyone starve. But a strike in theory is a voluntary act of workers banding together to seek higher wages and the like. It seems obvious that government-arranged subsidies intervene in the dispute on the side of labor. Such intervention can hardly help but lead to costlier and longer strikes.

There is room for more effective antitrust enforcement against business, too. Too often the enforcement agencies seem to opt for the "easy" cases, attacking companies simply because they are big. What's needed is more thoughtful consideration of business structure, with the stress not on size but on effects on competition.

The antitrust laws themselves could stand a fresh look. The Robinson-Patman Act actually works to discourage large companies from reducing prices; if they do, the government may allege that they are using "predatory" price cuts to force smaller firms out of business. The law actually was adopted primarily as an attack on chain food stores that were gradually forcing small single-unit groceries out of business.

As the laws are written now, a business may be in legal danger whatever it does with its prices. If it cuts prices, Robinson-Patman is waiting. If it keeps prices stable it may be colluding with other companies to fix prices. If it raises prices, it may be exhibiting illegal monopoly power.

Writing effective antitrust laws and enforcing them efficiently is no easy task, but inflation should provide the incentive to start.

The whole area of government regulation, railroads, antitrust, and everything else is long overdue for study. The Interstate Commerce Commission and other business regulators were supposedly set up to protect the public's interest. Too often they have wound up trying to protect businesses from competition.

As the experience of the Long Island and many other railroads has shown, the regulators sometimes are of little help to the regulated. The ICC often has barred railroads from cutting rates and offering new types of services for fear that they would damage competing types of carriers, such as truck and barge lines.

The ICC was set up in 1890 to check true abuses of railroad power. For many areas of the country, particularly in the West, the railroads were the only means of long-distance transportation. Competing railroads sometimes warred against one another, but usually they reached amicable agreements that allowed one or the other to charge whatever the public would bear.

In the 20th century, however, the railroads' monopoly power has been steadily eroded by the spread of trucks, automobiles, and airplanes. Yet government regulation has changed little since the days of monopoly.

Trucks were awarded to the ICC, but when airlines came only they got their own regulator, the Civil Aeronautics Board. Having a personal regulator has, over time, proved to be at best a mixed blessing.

Years ago, for instance, the CAB decided that Pan American World Airways should fly only international routes. In late 1974 there was general agreement in the industry that Pan Am would not have been in such dire financial straits (it was seeking a $10 million-a-month subsidy from the government) if it had been allowed to fly domestic routes.

Pan Am's primary U.S. competitor overseas, Trans World Airlines, was allowed to fly domestic routes. Other U.S. domestic lines, such as Northwest, have also been given international routes.

Louis Kohlmeier, who for years covered the regulatory agencies for the Washington bureau of *The Wall Street Journal,* finally wrote a book about the agencies. His conclusion: They did so much more harm than good that they should be abolished.

In early 1975 the Ford administration was not considering anything quite so drastic. Although administration officials were well aware of the inflationary impact of regulatory activity, they also knew that each of the agencies had built up its own constituency. Change will come slowly if it comes. Yet change is essential to long-run control of inflation, and certainly the country must not slide back into more controls.

Consider U.S. agriculture, which in 1973 and 1974 was not able to keep up with soaring demand in the United States and abroad, with the result that food prices led the inflation.

In comparison with the farms of other nations, U.S. agriculture is astonishingly efficient. In a 1974 study by the Committee for Economic Development, John L. Burns, a committee trustee, commented, "With respect to farm products, Russia uses half of its workers to underfeed its nation; China uses an even greater percentage." In contrast, the United States employs only 4 percent of its labor force on the farms—and the percentage is steadily decreasing.

Crop failures in the United States and abroad in 1973 and 1974 gave the impression that the surge in demand for U.S. farm products was a new development. Actually, the demand has grown steadily for many years.

Rising living standards and fast population growth have expanded the demand. In many of the developing countries, any crop failure can make the difference between substandard diets and mass starvation. High oil prices have been and will continue to make the problems worse, because energy is vital if less developed countries are to step up the output of their own farms.

Restraints on U.S. farm exports have been urged to hold down farm prices at home, but humanitarian reasons alone make such curbs objectionable. Economic reasons also argue against such restraints.

Clifton B. Lutrell, a St. Louis Federal Reserve Bank economist, put it this way in the October 1974 issue of the bank's *Review:*

"In the short run, domestic food prices would be lower with the quotas than without them. However, depending on whether or not there are substitutes for U.S. grain in foreign markets, the prices of U.S. imports could rise significantly." Less consumption, a euphenism for starvation, is of course one "substitute."

In any case, if foreigners didn't bid up the prices of the available U.S. supply the result would be reduced U.S. exports and a weaker dollar, raising the prices of U.S. imports. U.S. consumers would end up with more grain and fewer imports, and thus everyone would lose. In addition, U.S. export controls always raise the possibility of retaliatory measures, such as the actions of the oil cartel.

In the long run, export controls would be even more damaging. They would inhibit domestic production and cut incomes in agriculture and its supporting industries such as farm machinery. If controls were adopted only in emergencies, foreign nations wherever possible would look elsewhere for sources of supply, and long-term growth of the market would be stunted.

Controls, in sum, are not the way to change the market structure of the economy. Our best hope is to make the market system function as well as possible, using existing laws (or new ones, if necessary) to attack excessive concentrations of market power in either unions or business.

"Our economic understanding and models are simply not powerful enough to handle such a large and complex economic system better than the marketplace," C. Jackson Grayson wrote in the *Wall Street Journal* last year. Dr. Grayson, dean of the School of Business Administration at Southern Methodist University, knows something about controls: He ran the Price Commission under President Nixon.

The United States must start trying to make its present economic system more competitive—and carefully avoid new proposals to make it less so—if it is to hope to reach an era without inflation.

The inflationary bias in the economy is intensified by the "feedback" of past price changes onto the wage and pricemaking system through cost of living effects and expectations of future price changes. Employees resist real wage reductions and expect to be compensated for cost of living increases. Employers respond because they fear loss of morale and increased turnover and because they expect the price of competing products to rise.

James S. Duesenberry, Harvard University, at an American Enterprise Institute conference on inflation, May 1974.

chapter 15
Inflation expectations

The longer an inflation persists, the longer it takes to stop it. When inflation began speeding up in the United States in 1965, the nation had grown accustomed to relative price stability. Businessmen and consumers, like economists, tended to underestimate the inflation that was coming.

When expectations turn out to have been too low, there are two effects: Businessmen and consumers try to "catch up" with past inflation and they raise their expectations as to the future.

That's one reason why labor unions, amid the 1969–70 recession, were still pressing for substantial wage increases. Their previous contracts had failed to anticipate the price rise of the late 1960s. That's also one reason why businessmen went on raising prices, trying to catch up with past cost increases.

Rising expectations of inflation tend to encourage business speculation. When companies expect prices to continue to rise swiftly, they are more willing to borrow, since they feel that they will be able to pay off the loans in cheaper dollars. Interest rates tend to rise, since lenders try to protect themselves against the decline in the value of the dollar.

In the early stages of an inflation, consumers may splurge, trying to beat the higher prices they expect later on. As the inflation drags on, however, consumers grow more pessimistic. Consumer polls in the early 1970s were showing that people were beginning to equate inflation with hard times.

Such an appraisal is not unrealistic. Sooner or later an inflation will induce the government to take steps to check demand, and this has always led to a slowdown in the economy. Moreover, the inflation itself can lead to distortions in the economy that ultimately contribute to downturns.

Through much of 1974, for instance, inflation masked the true condition of business inventories so that many companies let their stocks reach excessive levels. When the economy slowed in the fall, the subsequent inventory-cutting was much more severe than it would have been if businessmen had had a clearer idea where they really stood.

Expectations, then, tend to lag behind the inflation at the start, so that some businessmen and consumers feel cheated by the price trend. As they try to catch up they help to speed the inflation. The expectations tend to linger on even after the government has begun to take the monetary-fiscal steps needed to check the inflation, with the result that the return to stability takes longer and costs more in terms of unemployment than otherwise would be the case.

Inflation can reduce unemployment only if the rate of price rise is underestimated by the workers. Employers go on raising prices and making higher profits, but workers' wage demands lag behind the price rise. The wage rate, in terms of constant dollars, thus is falling and employers hire more labor to increase output.

So if government policy makers want to reduce unemployment with expansionary financial policy, a prime requirement is to fool the people. But it's difficult to go on fooling the people forever. If an inflationary pattern persists for any length of time, the public will try to adjust to it. If inflation is accelerating, the public may overadjust, beginning to expect more inflation than is actually coming.

Overadjustment can have negative effects on employment. Rising real wage rates amid inflation will lead employers to try to hold down labor costs by stopping hiring or by laying off workers.

So how do we control inflation expectations?

In the long run, of course, the answer is that we control the expectations by controlling the inflation. If prices return to reasonable stability, and stay there for a while, expectations soon will be nothing to worry about. But how do we get from here to there?

Controls have been proposed as an answer. The idea is that controls hold down the actual rise of wages and prices, and thus deflate public expectations, while government is gradually applying the fiscal-monetary restraint that will really check the inflationary pressures.

There are several troubles with this approach, over and above the distortions controls can cause in the use of the economy's resources. For one thing, controls can work for an extended period only when market conditions are favorable—that is, when demand is not outrunning supply. For another thing, controls tend to worsen the expectations problem. When the idea of controls first arises, businessmen and labor unions try to beat the controls by raising prices and wages. A belief that controls soon will end can also distort business decisions, and after the restraints are removed business and labor try to make up for what they think they lost under controls. Fear that controls may be reimposed can lead to a push for even higher prices and wages.

Even more important, government finds it hard to accept the idea of financial restraint. Politicians must shelve or drop pet spending projects. And no matter how gradually the restraint is applied there are likely to be some bad side-effects, particularly on jobs. When controls are blurring inflation's effects for a time, there's a strong temptation for politicians to make the restraint so gradual that it really is no restraint at all.

What about indexing? The University of Chicago's Milton Friedman, among others, has urged indexing as an answer to the problem of expectations. Professor Friedman stresses that indexing is not a new idea: It was, for instance, urged by British economist Alfred Marshall in the late 19th century as a response to deflation, not inflation.

Professor Friedman stressed that indexing is not a cure for inflation but only a pain-killer, making it possible to apply gradually the financial restraint that will slow the rate of price rise.

What, exactly, is indexing?

The idea in brief is that all contracts involving deferred payments would be tied to a price index. Suppose a worker is paid $2 an hour and gets his check once a week. If the price index rises 1 percent during the week he will be paid his $2 plus 1 percent of $2, or a total of $2.02 an hour. The theory is that he will lose no purchasing power because of the inflation.

The same system would apply to contracts between businessmen. If the price index rose 10 percent between the time an order was placed and the goods were delivered, the price would be 10 percent higher. Savings accounts would be indexed, so that both principal and interest would rise in line with the price index.

Professor Friedman stresses that all indexing in the private economy should be on a voluntary basis. He and other supporters of the system, however, would like to see legislation compelling the federal government to index its tax system and its own securities.

As the progressive tax system now operates, inflation can push people into higher tax brackets even when their income—in terms of constant-value dollars—does not rise at all or perhaps even declines. Indexing the tax system would insure that an individual would pay taxes at a higher rate only if his "real" income rose.

Even while discussions of indexing were going on, the inflation of 1973–75 was pushing the system into more areas in the economy. Cost-of-living escalator clauses have appeared in some labor union contracts for more than a century and, as of late 1974, they covered more than 5 million workers. Such coverage was not always complete; in some cases, labor contracts limited the additional amounts the employers would have to pay. But at least wages did rise to some extent when prices rose.

Banks are writing an increasing number of business-loan contracts on a floating-rate basis, so that more inflation—and higher interest rates generally—will increase the banks' interest receipts. Business contracts for machinery and equipment often are being tied to price indexes.

Effective in January 1975, social security benefits are tied to a price index. Pensions to retired servicemen and federal employees are linked to price indexes. The longer the inflation persists at abnormal levels, the more widespread indexing is likely to be.

That, of course, won't tell us whether it's good or bad. An obvious good is that full indexing would protect the public from loss of income due to inflation. In the economy as it is, the impact of inflation is highly uneven, hurting some people more than others. The poor usually suffer most; in moderate, largely anticipated, inflation, the wealthy can usually protect themselves. In an inflation as severe and as unexpected as the United States had had in the early 1970s, however, inflation hurts the wealthy too.

The arguments for indexing go well beyond the fact that it provides an effective defense mechanism. As noted earlier, inflation expectations lead people to do many things, some of which are not necessarily desirable; indexing could reduce such responses.

If a consumer knew his wages would keep pace with the prices of cars and TV sets, for instance, there might be less panic buying. Businessmen would be able to operate at a steadier pace, less affected by the ups and downs of prices and interest rates.

Some proponents of indexing believe that it would promote greater stability in labor relations. If wages were geared to a price index, there would be no need for a union to demand large "catch-up" pay increases—or big boosts aimed at offsetting expected future inflation.

One very real advantage that is hard to measure: Businessmen and consumers would not have to spend so much time and resources in trying to guess what the price trend will be. Investments could be made safely without a fear that income and principal, or both, would be wiped out by inflation.

Indexing the tax system, in theory at least, would help to make sure that the government joined in the fight against inflation. The government would be one economic agent whose income would not automatically rise with prices. But the prices of the goods the government bought and the wages the government paid would of course rise. So the government, unless it was willing to accept steadily increasing deficits and presumably still more inflation, would have to cut spending programs or raise tax rates.

The objections against indexing might as well start at that point. Given the fact that the general public knows little about indexing, there is not going to be any great voter pressure on Congress to index the tax system. Without such pressure, it is unlikely, to put it very mildly, that Congress will ever choose to put the government in that sort of box—even though tax-indexing legislation was introduced in 1974.

Continuing with the purely practical and political objections: selection of an index poses some problems of equity. The consumer price index, the price gauge most frequently used, measures prices of goods and services most frequently bought by wage earners and clerical workers. It may provide relatively less protection to persons in other groups.

If indexation was voluntary in the private sector, some groups with limited economic power might have little or no protection at all. Price trends, moreover, vary throughout the economy. In some indexed contracts now in existence, several indexes are involved—a different one to cover each different category of goods.

If indexes were applied to home mortgages—a key part of every proposal—savings and loan associations still would be left with a lot of fixed-rate contracts. There would have to be some sort of massive government subsidy to clear the decks for indexing.

Many of these fixed-rate mortgages were written at rates under the market as it existed in early 1975; others were written at higher rates. If indexing is to offer a situation where both borrowers and lenders are protected these loans would have to be replaced—and one party or the other would have to be given an incentive to alter the contract.

The likelihood that protection would be uneven means that inflationary expectations would persist to some extent at least. If an indexing system began to provide rather full protection for everyone, though, it could lessen the government's incentive to do anything at all about inflation. The chief pressure for anti-inflation action now comes from a public that feels its real earnings are being eroded by rising prices; if the erosion is not occurring, will political leaders worry as much about inflation?

As for the argument that indexing would smooth labor relations, nothing in the system will prevent labor organizations from seeking to improve the real incomes of their members. Indexing could remove one major item of contention but it would by no means assure labor peace.

When inflation is heating up, indexing is likely to build up the heat more rapidly. Every rise in the price index will assure a rise in wages and incomes, which are somebody else's costs, and thus will put still more upward pressure on prices.

If and when inflation began to cool off, however, indexing would become an aid. Without it, workers would go on demanding higher wages to offset expected inflation and businessmen would be slow to reduce prices because they would expect costs to go on rising.

If indexing was in place, workers would know that their wages would rise in pace with whatever inflation still occurred. Businessmen would know that their costs would rise more slowly as the general inflation slowed down.

The cases for and against indexing, then, are rather mixed. As a practical matter, as long as inflation persists, indexing will continue to spread through the economy. Given the political realities, though, anything like full and complete indexing seems a long way off.

Incomplete indexing, of the sort we have now, simply makes it all the clearer that inflation hurts some people more than it does others—and thus contributes to social unrest and pressure on government to do something about the inflation.

In sum, full indexing is not an available alternative for dealing with the problems of inflation expectations, and it would not provide a perfect solution if it were available. The only way to eliminate inflation expectations is, once again, to eliminate the inflation.

This simply cannot be done painlessly, especially not when the inflation has built up over a long period, as it had in the United States in the late 1960s and early 1970s. A primary requisite is strong governmental leadership that will make it clear that government does indeed intend to eliminate inflation.

"Gradualism" has been given a bad name by some of the economic policies of the Nixon administration, but there remains much to be said for it: slowly reducing the growth rate of the money supply and slowly increasing the degree of fiscal restraint.

If policy is clearly announced and consistently followed, it will in time reduce expectations of future inflation. As for easing the pain, some of the steps suggested in Chapter 13 would help. Along the way, too, unemployment compensation would have to provide a cushion.

There is no magic way to handle inflation expectations.

With old inflation riding the headlines, I have read till I'm bleary-eyed, and I can't get head from tails of the whole thing. We are living in an age of explanations, and plenty of them, too, but no two things that's been done to us has been explained twice the same way—by even the same man.

Will Rogers, in a newspaper column first published in January 1934.

chapter 16
What we can do

There's considerable irony in the fact that Will Rogers's remark was made at a time when the country had just experienced one of its worst-ever periods of deflation, not inflation; between 1929 and 1933 the Consumer Price Index fell by 24 percent.

It's true that prices had begun to perk up a bit by early 1934. Moreover, the government was chopping away at the gold content of the dollar with the deliberate aim of encouraging some price inflation. Even amid the miseries of the early 1930s, the situation had Will and other people worried.

Obviously enough, worry is not a sufficient response to inflation. No one in America has ever had to live with inflation as severe and prolonged as that which has afflicted the United States in the late 1960s and the 1970s. How does the citizen survive?

Right at the start, let's make it clear that there is no sure-fire way to beat the kind of inflation the United States has had in recent years. The best financial advice for an average American amid inflation is actually good financial advice at any time.

Inflation leaves less room for nonessentials and pure unadulterated waste. The prices of the things we must have—food, clothing, and shelter—are rising all the time. So the first chore of every person is to be sure he has enough money for the essentials.

This may mean driving the old car another year. But whatever the impression left by the inflation summits of 1974, this sort of self-denial is not aimed primarily at "whipping" inflation now; it's aimed at letting you survive inflation now.

Sometimes the best tactic may be to buy a new car. What each individual and family should do depends on its circumstances. If the upkeep of the old car is mounting, if payments on existing debts are low, a new car may save money.

Within reasonable limits, debt has its advantages amid high inflation, since the debtor is paying off his obligation in dollars that are worth progressively less. Those reasonable limits include the fact that the debtor should be working at a job where his wage or salary is likely to rise more or less in step with the inflation.

In other words, an American should simply live sensibly. That means that he should have an eye on the future. Present and prospective inflation (those inflation expectations again) must be taken into account in planning for children's educations, retirement, and other future outlays.

But what do you do with the funds you set aside for that uncertain future?

Some advisers have touted gold as a refuge. Americans were not legally allowed to own gold until 1975, but they could and some did buy gold-mining stocks. Anyone who bought gold in 1973 or before was well ahead of the game in early 1975.

But, as any intelligent gold speculator knows, the gold market is highly volatile. Only a tiny fraction of the world's supply trades in that market; the vast majority of it is locked up in nations' currency reserves. So relatively small buy or sell orders can send the market swiftly in one direction or the other.

In the wake of the sharp rise in world oil prices, some economists think the gold market has acquired a large new element of instability. None of the nations facing big new oil import bills will use gold at the official price—$42.22 an ounce—to pay for oil. But countries now can revalue their gold in terms of the free-market price, which is several times the official level.

Moreover, there is nothing to prevent some countries from selling some of their gold in the free market. In early 1975 the United States did so in an effort to head off imports of gold when U.S. citizens were allowed to buy the metal. As it turned out, the public demand in the United States was limited.

One reason why Americans, at least initially, showed little interest in gold was price; gold may have seemed attractive at $50, $75, or even $100 an ounce, but $175 or higher looked forbidding. In addition, bankers and economists were careful to stress that although gold may be beautiful it pays no interest and can be expensive to store.

Real estate, antiques, paintings, stamps and other forms of real property may offer some protection for some investors. But such investments require special knowledge and provide limited liquidity. Real estate, if it is rented or leased, may provide current yield—but this involves the investor in the uncertainties of a business operation. And it is hardly necessary to add the real estate business is at its most uncertain in an environment of high inflation.

Nonetheless real property can appreciate in line with inflation or, if you're lucky, even faster. Persons with special knowledge of certain types of property, or with access to such knowledge, may find such investments comforting.

The lack of liquidity in real-property investments is not something to be taken lightly. An individual who has to sell an antique, a painting, or even a vacant lot in a hurry is likely to get much less for it than he would receive if he were able to wait for the "right" price.

Liquidity is, of course, what securities markets do provide. The experience of 1973–75, however, should at last bury the old notion that common stocks are a reliable hedge against inflation. The National Bureau of Economic Research in 1974 published a study by Columbia University economist Phillip Cagan, who concluded that stocks can be such a hedge—if the investor can wait long enough.

Between 1939 and 1948 stock values rose by an average of 2.7 percent a year, well below the average 6 percent rise in consumer prices. Between 1948 and 1969, however, the average rise in stock values was 9 percent, compared with an average consumer price increase of only 2.1 percent. Between early 1973 and late 1974, while inflation was racing into double-digit territory, the Dow-Jones Industrial Average of 30 blue-chip stocks fell from over 1000 to under 600. The average investor who bought common stock as an inflation hedge in early 1973, obviously enough, only complicated his current problems.

A study by Fields, Grant & Co., a Menlo Park, California investment counseling firm, suggests that stocks are a good short-term hedge against inflation only when there isn't much inflation.

"With high inflation rates," the firm says, "stock prices will usually deteriorate, even though earnings growth may not. This is because stock yields, like bond yields, will rise in order to compensate the buyer for the expected decline in the real purchasing power of that stock or bond on resale to the next buyer."

If it's any comfort to the general public, professional investors also find it hard to keep inflation from eroding their dollars. In 1973 and 1974, while the stock market headed south, many of the professionals put growing proportions of their money into short-term and fixed-income investments. But some went on buying common stock, confident (hopeful?) that everything would work out eventually.

Anyone who buys common stock during an inflationary period naturally should stress quality; he wants a company with a chance of weathering the uncertainty. In similar periods in the past, utility and bank stocks often have been considered to be relatively safe.

But the severity of the inflation of 1973–75, together with the quadrupling of oil prices, created serious problems for the utilities. They faced sharply higher fuel costs, and these costs were seldom immediately offset by rate increases. When giant Consolidated Edison Company of New York was forced to omit a dividend in early 1974, investors worried more about all utilities, although some of Con Ed's problems were unique.

Similarly, the troubles of New York's Franklin National Bank in 1974 caused worry about banks generally. Franklin, which lost millions in foreign exchange operations, was eventually absorbed by a consortium of European banks. Although Franklin's problems, like Con Ed's, were in part its own, the banking system in general was stretched thin in early 1975. Only by borrowing heavily were the banks able to keep up with continued high loan demand.

174

The difficulty of assessing individual common stocks, or even groups of stocks, explained why so many investors leaned toward fixed-income securities, especially short-term issues.

In periods of uncertainty, most investors are not eager to commit funds to long-term investments such as corporate bonds. "Interest rates may look high now," said one analyst in late 1974, "but I can remember when 5 percent looked like a high rate."

If an investor sticks entirely to Treasury bills and other short-term securities, though, that means that he must spend a great deal of time on his investments—or pay someone else to do so. Treasury bills mature in three months, and when they do they stop paying interest. Short-term rates, moreover, are highly volatile; when an individual reinvests, he may have to accept a lower rate.

If you decide to manage your own money, the first requirement is to be completely honest with yourself. Any program you select should be designed to fit your abilities—and the time that you have to use those abilities.

The investor who decides to let someone manage his money needs to remember that professional advisers vary widely in competence. There is no simple way to find the one who is best for you: The only hope is to solicit the advice of friends or lawyers or bankers you know and trust.

In a general way, a small investor should avoid a large investment advisory firm; his account can get lost. As noted earlier, too, professional investment advice will not provide sure-fire answers to all the questions of an inflated economy; the pros have been as puzzled as the amateurs.

Whether you manage your own money or let someone else do it, you have to be realistic about your own situation. Can you really afford to gamble that the price of gold will go on going up?

You'll be better off losing small portions of your purchasing power in safe investments whose yields do not match the inflation rate than you will if you lose your principal in speculation. Every investor, in an inflationary period or at any other time, needs to do some careful risk analysis, and the smart man errs on the side of being too conservative.

The first essential, to repeat, is to budget carefully for current expenses, in the full knowledge that those expenses are growing with the inflation. That means keeping enough cash, or cash equivalent, on hand to pay the landlord, the grocer, and the utility company.

With or without inflation, the individual should keep as little money as possible in the form of cash or a checking account. Banks and savings and loan associations offer day-of-deposit-to-day-of-withdrawal savings accounts that pay interest and provide no penalties if funds must be withdrawn. In determining how much cash to hold, of course, the individual must determine for himself what value he puts on his own convenience; even using a bank savings account involves some time and trouble.

If you are middle-aged or younger and can afford short-term risks, quality common stocks will still provide good long-term protection against inflation. Some fortunate souls may even be able to beat inflation by beating the market; picking the Xerox or the IBM of the future. But for every Xerox of the future there are probably a few dozen Four Seasons Nursing Homes and National Student Marketings. Speculation can provide fun and profit—or disaster.

The investor who wants less risk—and less long-term protection against inflation—can choose high-grade corporate bonds.

Some such securities, issued in earlier years at interest rates below the levels of the 1970s, now sell at substantial discounts, providing respectable rates of return and an almost-sure capital gain when the bonds are redeemed at par at maturity.

In general, the sort of yields available on relatively safe investments will not protect anyone against the double-digit inflation that existed in the United States in late 1974. In part this is a reflection of the fact that the public does not expect double-digit inflation to continue forever; if it did, yields would adjust to higher levels. If the public is right in its optimism, budgeting and investing carefully can provide the individual long-term protection.

If the public wants to make sure that it is right, however, it will have to support the kind of political leadership that will curb inflation at its source: government.

The fight against inflation cannot be waged without costs, but the consequences of not ending the inflationary spiral would impose a far heavier burden on the long-run economic welfare of the American people."

Andrew F. Brimmer, former Member, Federal Reserve Board of Governors, in a speech in August 1974.

chapter 17
Summary and conclusions

M ost Americans seem to recognize that the government is chiefly responsible for inflation. In a working democracy, though, the government is us. Our political "leaders" are more often likely to be followers, trying to please most of their constituents most of the time. Politicians rise and fall in the short run, and the short-run effects of inflationary policies are often pleasant for most people. If we let the government lead us from one inflationary plateau to one even higher, we deserve the inflation we get.

How do we get out of this mess?

First, we need to support the kind of political candidates who are willing to look at the broad, long-run effects of spending programs, subsidies, and other measures. Government is continually besieged by special-interest proposals that promise gains for certain groups. A wonderful example of this sort of legislation came up in late 1974, with the nation deep in its energy problems and double-digit inflation.

The proposal was simple enough: A specified percentage of all the oil imported into the United States would have to be carried in U.S. tankers. Everyone seemed to recognize that the United States didn't have enough tankers to meet the requirement and thus would have to build more at costs exceeding those of foreign shipyards. The net result would have been to push the cost of imported oil, which already had more than quadrupled in a year, to still higher levels.

At the same time, though, the bill promised some jobs for U.S. seamen and shipyard workers. So the measure whizzed through both houses of Congress. Fortunately, President Gerald Ford had the wisdom and fortitude to veto it. Government is going to have to forgo measures that benefit the few at the expense of the many.

Of course, if you happen to be a cattleman it's easy for you to oppose that sort of special deal for seamen and shipyard workers. And if you happen to be a seaman, it may be easy for you to object when President Ford arranges "voluntary" limitations on meat imports to help promote higher prices for cattlemen—and all consumers, obviously.

Special-interest legislation is scattered through the statute books and much of it tends to push up prices. Other measures tend to limit supply and thus are also inflationary; price control on natural gas, for instance, has tended to discourage the search for new sources of the fuel.

Even legislation that benefits broad sections of the population or serves a general public interest must be considered in the light of its inflationary impact. Measures to protect the environment and to aid automobile and factory safety are needed, yet even their benefits must be balanced against their inflationary costs.

Even more fundamentally, we need to recognize that government cannot solve all the world's problems. In recent decades the growing prosperity of the United States has made it possible for the country to worry more about social and environmental problems.

But it may be that our reach has exceeded our grasp. Consider, for instance, health care. Adequate health care for all Americans is surely a desirable national goal, but even desirable goals often must be sought in an economic way. In recent years the pursuit of this particular goal has been anything but economic.

Writing in *The Public Interest* in 1972, Columbia University economist James W. Kuhn recalls that in 1965, when new health programs for the poor and aged were introduced, "the nation's expenditures for personal health care were $35 billion; three years later, the total had reached $50 billion, of which the federal government was providing $10 billion annually."

> The funds flowed far faster than doctors, hospital staffs and other medical personnel could adjust. Though many persons benefitted from the programs, their purposes were not always well served. . . . Those with the lowest incomes were rationed out of the market as wages and prices jumped upward in a classic inflationary response.

Federal, state, and local governments also have been something less than fully successful in their efforts to solve other problems—in education, in housing, and in numerous other areas. Frequently a major difficulty has been that governments have paid too little attention to the fact that resources are limited and, in some way, must be allocated among the various competing demands.

The idea that the country can rush right in and do everything all at once leads to vast amounts of waste, frustration, and confusion. When taxes don't provide enough money to pay all the bills, the government tries to think of other taxes. When that approach doesn't work, the government may resort to the ultimate tax: inflation.

Inflation is represented by a rise in the general price level. Oil price increases dictated by the Arabs or food price increases caused by poor harvests or government price supports are not in and of themselves inflationary. If the Federal Reserve System does not accommodate such price increases by stepping up the growth rate of the money supply, the increases affect only relative prices, not general prices. The public pays more for oil and food but cuts down its spending on other items.

In recent years the Federal Reserve has been very accommodative. Large portions of the growing federal debt wind up in the portfolio of the Fed and thus increase the reserves of the banking system and its ability to expand the money supply.

What I've tried to do in this book is to sketch what the resulting inflation has meant to American individuals and institutions, to explain how we got into this situation, and to describe how we just possibly may get out of it.

As Andrew Brimmer says, getting out of the mess won't be easy. In early 1975 it was already apparent that the gains being made against the inflation were being made only at the cost of what was the most severe business decline since the depression of the 1930s.

What makes the attack on inflation especially difficult is that no one can say just exactly what it will cost. There is no neat tradeoff between inflation and unemployment. A political leader cannot decide to accept two more percentage points of unemployment to get two less percentage points of inflation—or vice versa. The early 1970s have shown us that not only can high unemployment and high inflation go together, but that more of the one doesn't automatically bring us less of the other. No politician openly endorses inflation, but many shrink from the political hazards of ending it.

Part of the problem is simply the size and complexity of the economy. We know a lot more about how the economy operates than we did a generation ago, but our knowledge is still far fram complete. Part of the problem is the statistics—usually lagging well behind events, often revised, sometimes blurred by the inflation itself. It's difficult to measure what's going on, as well as to gauge the effects of inflation remedies.

Moreover, the environment keeps changing all the time. More women and teen-agers join the labor force, the government continues to make unemployment less painful, public expectations keep rising. The government alters the workings of the economy with varying forms of regulation, changes in the tax laws, tariffs, and other trade restrictions. Some economists complain that the economy doesn't work the way it used to, and in a sense that's true: today's economy simply is different from yesterday's.

So the risks are great. But we do know how to end inflation; government ends it simply by restraining its spending and its creation of money. If we want to end it we must accept the risks and move ahead.

Obviously enough, that's a tough choice politically. But once the nation is stuck with double-digit inflation, what is the alternative? Can we learn to live with inflation?

Perhaps we could, if the inflation rate were relatively stable at 4 percent or 5 percent a year. But no nation as yet has been able to hold the inflation rate stable; historically, inflation always has been either accelerating or slowing down.

If inflation could be stabilized, or even if its fluctuations were always predictable, the damage it does would largely disappear. Everyone would adjust to it and life would go on. As we have seen, indexing is a plan to adjust to inflation, but political and practical problems make it unlikely that indexing can protect everyone.

So if we accept inflation in our future, the probability is that it will be a fluctuating inflation. Such an inflation will continue to "threaten the very foundations of our society." Local and state governments, unable to cope with inflation on their own, will lean increasingly on the federal government. Private institutions will come to depend more and more on the public purse.

Both consumers and businessmen will use large amounts of resources in trying to predict inflation and to hedge themselves against it. In a stable economy, such resources could be used in more productive ways.

Inflation naturally will increase business uncertainties and encourage speculation. Long-range planning, of the sort that is needed to provide future jobs, will be discouraged. Who can be happy about planning a new factory for 1980 if he can't have the faintest notion of costs and selling prices?

All along, of course, inflation will increase the disparities in our society. Debt is in effect rewarded, thrift punished. Some members of society, usually those who are already most affluent, are best able to find ways to protect themselves.

It is, in sum, the sort of world that few of us would admire. The way to avoid it is clear. The only question is whether we will take it.

Index

Index

190

Rockefeller, David, 12
Rogers, Will, 168–69
Roosevelt administration, 92, 137–38
Rueff, Jacques, 64

S

Savings and loan associations, 5, 48–50
Schmiedeskamp, Jay, 9, 27, 29
Second Bank of the United States, 15
Securities and Exchange Commission, 35
Shadow Open Market Committee, 133
Shultz, George, 66, 142–43
Simon, William, 10
Sony television sets, 17, 61
Stock market, 7, 50–51, 69
Survey Research Center, 9, 26–27
Sutterly, Elmer J., 23

T

Taft-Hartley Act, 149
Taxes, local property, 22
Tax reduction (1964), 95–96
Taxes, sales and income, 23
Tax surcharge (1968), 97
Terborgh, George, 34
Tobin, James, 90, 99
Trade, free, 148
Trans World Airlines, 154
Treasury accord, 128
Treasury borrowing, 138–40
Truman administration, 91

U

Unemployment, 82–83, 103–11
  natural rate, 108
  inflation expectations, 160–61
Unemployment compensation, 107
Unions, labor, 149–52
  building trades, 86
United Auto Workers, 105
U.S. Congress, 14, 80–81, 95
U.S. Steel, 95

V

Vietnam war, 53, 60, 96

W

Wage-price controls, 40, 69–71, 79, 147
  August 1971, 98–99
  role in economy, 115–24
  wartime, 116–17, 122
  World War II aftermath, 5
Wage-price guidelines, 94–95, 118, 120–21
Wall Street Journal, 95
Wallich, Henry, 146, 149–50
Wholesale Price Index, 16–18
  defined, 17
Wicksell, Knut, 87–88
World War I, 15
World War II, 4–5, 15

X

Xerox, 175